PUNITIVE DAMAGES

PUNITIVE DAMAGES

JIM LIVELY

MERRIMACK MEDIA
Boston, Massachusetts

Tic

Library of Congress Control Number: 2016944388

ISBN: print: 978-1-939166-97-5
ISBN: ebook: 978-1-939166-98-2

Illustrations by Jim Lively

Published by Merrimack Media, Boston, Massachusetts
June 2016

Dedication

*This book is dedicated to Jenny Lobaugh Thomas
and others who volunteer for Weimaraner Rescue
of North Texas and similar organizations around
the country that place rescue dogs into loving
homes.*

Contents

1

Punitive Damages

What's that terrible smell? The pungent aroma of disinfectant permeated the room. *Where am I?* Suddenly, I woke up from what seemed like a very deep sleep. Try as I might, my eyes could not focus. My head was throbbing, everything was blurred, and colors were swirling around. I sensed that I was lying on something very hard. Although I was cold, I felt an intensely bright light dangling just over my body. *What happened?* Slowly, as my eyes began to adjust to my surroundings, I started to make out the figures of people who were milling around where I was lying. My keen sense of smell was working overtime to compensate for my eyes lack of clarity. Ever so slightly, I raised my head off of the hard surface and tried to get a better look at my surroundings. Apparently, my movement did not go undetected. A woman who wore a white coat said in my general direction, "So, you decided to join us?"

My eyes began to focus. I could tell that I was positioned on some kind of table, which was in the middle of a sanitized, scented room. The smell of an assortment of various chemicals continued to overwhelm me.

As the woman walked over to me, I could smell a lovely sweet scent amid the otherwise objectionable odors. The nearer she got to me, the stronger the scent became. She extended her hand in my direction and lightly patted my head. As she briefly hovered over me, I smelled a slight hint of cinnamon on her sleeve. The woman must have recently eaten something sprinkled with cinnamon. *I love the smell of cinnamon.* She patted my head and then took some kind of instrument from around her nicely scented neck, which she pressed on the left side of my chest. She kept her hand pressed down on the instrument for several seconds. Smiling at me, she said, "Well, your heart beat is normal." Then she took two fingers and started to examine my teeth. She moved from the left side of my mouth feeling each one of my teeth in the process. When she reached the right side of my mouth she stopped and said, "Tom, come and look at this."

I heard a bit of a commotion and smelled a strong musky fragrance that I could not identify. The fragrance was attached to a heavyset man. He wore a white coat similar to that of the nice-smelling woman. As he moved closer to the right side of my head, I also smelled an aroma of coffee emanating from his mouth.

The cinnamon-scented woman then moved her fingers on the upper side of my mouth. When she did, I winced in pain and let out a slight cry. "Poor girl, she lost her right canine and the one premolar next to it."

Tom responded, "She certainly paid dearly for her little adventure."

The woman then removed her hand from my mouth and patted my head. "Well, she won't win any beauty contests, but it shouldn't affect her ability to eat. I suspect that her upper lip will occasionally find its way in the gap where the two teeth were and detract from her beautiful appearance."

She must be mistaken, I am beautiful. I am certain—everyone tells me that I am beautiful, but I can't remember why. I decided that I'd had enough of the conversation, and attempted to shift my legs underneath me so that I could stand up. At that moment, I felt an incredibly sharp pain shoot through my lower right extremity. At that moment, the woman grabbed my hindquarters so I could not move.

"No sweetie, you aren't going anywhere." She then spoke to Tom, "Help hold her down while I examine her leg. I think she might have a fracture."

Again, I smelled the musky odor that radiated from Tom's neck region, which was coupled with the coffee from his breath. He was a strong man and had no trouble holding me motionless. The woman began running her hand over my leg and stopped at my knee. She then applied just a slight amount of pressure just under the joint in my leg, which again caused me to wince and yelp with pain.

"I think she has a slight fracture here. Even if we X-ray it, there's nothing further we can do to treat it beyond letting it rest and heal naturally. She might always have a slight limp. It's too early to tell." The woman with the lovely scent looked down at me and smiled, "You've been through enough for today. Tom is going to take you to the back and let you get some rest."

Tom responded, "Judging by her injuries, she must've been on the losing end of an encounter with a car or truck."

Tom reached underneath me with his strong hands and easily lifted me from the table. He was very gentle for such a large man. He definitely knew how to lift me without hurting me. Tom carried me into an adjoining room and placed me in a small confined area with a nice warm bed. He then left the room and closed the door behind him. I glanced around the room. There were other similar confined areas and beds similar to where Tom placed me, but no one else was here. The light was not as bright in this room as the one I had just left. There was still a smell of chemicals, but not as pungent as the other room. The woman was right: I'd had enough for the day. I was very tired. I closed my eyes and could hear the murmur of voices from the other room. My eyelids grew heavy and I surrendered to sleep.

*****

I am not sure how long I was asleep, but when I opened my eyes I looked around and noticed all the lights were turned off and it was very quiet. The only noise that I could hear was the humming of some appliance that occupied the space directly across from my bed. I raised my head to look around. When I turned my head to the right, I immediately identified a familiar odor. I smelled a tinge of bacon in the air. I absolutely love bacon. It is the perfect food! It emits this lovely aroma that permeates the entire house when it is cooking. I cannot recall when I last had bacon. In fact, I cannot recall almost anything before waking up in the room next door. I can sort all this out in due time. Right now, I'm hungry.

Although my leg hurt, I could still apply a bit of weight on it. When I stood up, I noticed a plate set just inside my area. The smell of bacon grew stronger as I approached the plate. I leaned over and sniffed. While the presentation was not spectacular, whatever this was smelled good enough. I took a slight bite of food and remembered the right side of my mouth was extremely sore. As I took each bite, I immediately shifted it with my tongue to the left side of my mouth so that I could chew without too much pain. I perfected this technique by the end of my dinner. It was not the best meal that I have ever had, but I managed to clean my plate despite the pain.

The food gave me some strength and clarity. I decided to return to my bed and assess my situation. I remembered the woman with the lovely scent and the cinnamon on her sleeve. *Some of that cinnamon sprinkled on top of my food tonight would have certainly helped the presentation and flavor.* My thoughts drifted to her comments, "Poor girl, she lost her right canine and the premolar next to it." I shifted my tongue to the upper right side of my mouth. Indeed, there was a sensitive vacuous space where my two teeth previously resided. *How did I lose my teeth?* I had no recollection whatsoever. *And my leg, how did I hurt it? Was it at the same time as my teeth? So many mysteries!*

Fatigue began to get the best of me. It was late and my stomach was full. I felt content in a strange way. These folks were obviously nice. They gave me food and a warm bed for the night. *Tomorrow is another day. I will remember what happened then and be on my way.*

*****

I must have slept the entire night because when I awoke, I could see some sunlight filtering in underneath the door. Soon, I began to hear voices in the other room. Tom opened the door to my room, and as soon as the door swung open, I instantly smelled his musky odor. He looked at me and smiled, "It looks like you found the dinner that I prepared for you. At least you haven't lost your appetite." He came over and helped me to my feet and said, "Come on follow me, it's time for you to stretch your legs and get a little fresh air."

I followed Tom through the same room with the strong chemical smells where I was yesterday. He unlocked an exterior door and held it open for me. Although I was noticeably limping and in pain, walking felt comforting. It was a beautiful sunny day. I walked away from Tom to the other side of the fenced yard and sniffed around a bit. There were all kinds of competing odors. I was so enthralled with all the various scents that I forgot Tom was even there. Nonetheless, he did not forget about me and shouted, "Be a good girl and take care of your business."

Did he really mean what I think he meant? Does he really think that I would go to the bathroom while he stands there and watches? I shot him my meanest looking glare in my arsenal of expressions.

He laughed out loud. "Listen, girl, you don't look too threatening with your right lip sucked into the gap where you lost your two teeth."

My facial expression softened. I think Tom could sense that he had hurt my feelings. He said, "Okay, have it your way. I'll give you some privacy." He laughed out loud again and reentered the building.

I could tell from all the odors permeating the yard that I was certainly not the first one to, "take care of my business." I sniffed around a bit more and found a shady spot underneath a Live Oak tree and squatted down. My sore leg throbbed with pain, but I managed to finish. It did feel good to finally relieve myself. I couldn't remember the last time I went to the bathroom. It certainly wasn't outside in this kind of yard though. *I wish I could remember what happened to me?*

I snooped around the yard a bit longer and walked over to the door where Tom reentered the building. Something triggered in my memory that prompted me to scratch my nails on the door. I repeated this maneuver several times before the door swung open. Tom opened the door and gazed down at me. He said, "Girl, I didn't forget about you. In fact, you'll find your breakfast waiting for you in the other room."

Tom had not even finished his sentence before I could smell the intoxicating aroma of bacon, drifting in from the room where I had spent the previous night. I limped briskly to the other room. As I approached the source of the aroma, I could tell it was exactly the same dish and presentation that Tom had prepared for my dinner. *Tom isn't too creative, but he does mean well.* I sniffed around the plate a bit before taking a bite of food. Methodically, I followed the same practice as I had done eating my dinner the night before. Other than my dinner last night, I am not sure when I had last eaten.

After breakfast, I felt a little drowsy. I knew I should probably be on my way, but for the life of me, I had no recollection of anything before waking yesterday on the hard table in the other room. All I knew for certain was that I was weak from various injuries. For the first time since my arrival, I noticed a full-length mirror on the wall adjacent to where I had my breakfast. I had been so intent on eating, that I failed to see anything but my breakfast. I limped over and positioned myself directly in front of the mirror. I gasped at what I saw.

My reflection revealed that I had lost weight. My ribs protruded from beneath my skin. The woman with the lovely scent was correct, my right lip did get stuck in the space were my two missing teeth previously resided. When I opened my mouth, the lip would return to its normal position. If I inhaled through my mouth, the lip would suck back into the gap. I sighed. *What had happened to me?*

I limped back to where Tom had made my bed and entered the confined space. I turned around a bit before I settled upon a perfect spot to rest. I had to make sure that I lay just right on my left side so that there was no pressure on my injured leg. It was relatively quiet except for voices that carried over from an adjacent room. I drifted off to sleep.

2

The Gray Brute

_____

I must have been asleep for a couple of hours when I heard noises from the room next door. People were shouting and it sounded like furniture was being moved around. I recognized the voice of the woman with the lovely scent. She was speaking in a very loud tone, "Tom, don't try and lift him onto the table! He is too large for the two of us! I'll examine him down here. Just try to calm him down so he won't break anything. He's a big fella!"

I could tell from the groaning going on that Tom was struggling with whatever it was that he was trying to keep calm. After a few more moments, it became relatively still next door. I heard Tom say, "There, I think he's finally calmed down enough for you to come closer and examine him."

I heard the woman with the lovely scent say, "Okay, big boy, take it easy. I'm not going to hurt you. I just have to check you out." A few minutes passed, and then she said, "Okay, big boy, you look fine—quite a bit overweight, but no worse for wear. Tom, I want to take a blood sample so we can test for worms." Suddenly, I heard even more commotion from the room. It sounded like a chair got knocked over. The woman shouted, "Hold him, Tom, I'm almost done!" Apparently, Tom was successful because then the woman said, "Okay, I've got it. We're all done, big fella. Tom, take him and put him in the large crate next to our young lady patient."

When I heard her say, "next to our young lady patient," I hoped that she was not referring to me. I do not like having to share my room with anyone else, especially someone that sounded as out of control as this "big fella."

Just then, the door swung open and my peace and solitude came to a screeching halt. At first, all I could see was Tom. He appeared to be struggling as he shouted, "No, no, no! In here, come on!" I saw Tom holding on to some kind of leash, which was very taut, and that he was engaged in a tug of war with something on the other end of the leash. Finally, without warning, the leash slackened, which surprised Tom. He lost his footing and fell backward. Tom landed on his back, causing this huge gray brute to leap to his feet and bound into my room. He ran directly over to where I had eaten breakfast and stepped in my bowl. The force from his foot struck the bowl so violently that it went sailing across the room. It bounced off the wall and the refrigerator before coming to a resting place upside down in the middle of the room.

The gray brute stood and stared at the bowl as if mesmerized by its maneuvers. He then came to his senses and cast a glance in my direction. I was still lying down with my head positioned on a blanket near the open door of my confined space. Without warning, the gray brute came charging directly toward me. He hit the open doorway at a dead run, but he was so large that instead of clearing the opening, his shoulder caught the side of my crate. This collision caused my crate to spin 180 degrees clockwise and was so forceful that I was ejected from my confined space. I ended up in the middle of the room next to my breakfast bowl, wondering what the gray brute was going to do next.

Before the gray brute could turn around, Tom grabbed the leash that hung from his neck and said, "Big boy, you need to behave. You're going to hurt somebody. Let's go over here and get comfortable in this crate. You're big, but you should fit in it nicely." To my surprise, the gray brute cooperated fully with Tom's directions and entered the oversized crate without any more drama.

Tom looked over at me and said, "Girl, are you okay? Come here, I'll readjust your crate for you." Tom repositioned my crate in its proper place and motioned with his hand for me to come to him. I gingerly got up to my feet and took an opportunity to stretch my legs before walking over to him. After I entered my crate, Tom shut the door behind me and whispered, "I know you're a good girl, but I am closing this door behind you for your own protection." He then handed me a bacon treat through the bars of my door. I almost took his hand off going for the treat. With all the excitement, I had not even smelled the treat before he handed it to me. Usually, I can smell a treat coming a mile away. Well, I do have a keen sense of smell.

I shot a glance over to the gray brute. He was lying with his back pressed against the side of his crate. I could tell by his measured breathing that he was asleep. *How could he go from a raging lunatic one minute to being sound asleep the next? He is quite an interesting character.*

The gray brute and I were pretty much left alone for the remainder of the day. Periodically, Tom would come in and lead one of us outside to the closed yard to stretch our legs and take care of business. The difference in the way each of us responded to Tom was remarkable. I was the cool and calculated one. When Tom approached my crate and unlocked my door, I would hesitate inside even after he called to me, "Come on girl, let's get some fresh air."

Why rush things? Sure, I can't recall my past, but I know I must be of aristocratic stock. There's no need to rush when the hired help is performing some task for my benefit. Tom is nice to me, but that's just the natural order of things between the haves and have-nots.

On the other hand, while I only casually glanced up when the door opened, the gray brute responded as if the world were coming to an end. He immediately jumped up and started barking at the top of his lungs. You could hear him from blocks away. As Tom approached his crate, he would start turning around rapidly, causing the entire room to vibrate. The entire time he was spinning and vibrating, he continued vocalizing his hideous bark. The moment Tom unlatched the crate's door, the gray brute lunged forward. Tom had learned his lesson. This time he quickly stepped to the side so as not to be flattened by the beast. *This creature has obviously had a different upbringing than mine. He certainly does not derive from regal roots. I most certainly did.*

Tom always made sure we were never left alone. He methodically kept us separated. As I was out stretching my legs in the outer yard, Tom would let the gray brute out of his crate and feed him. When the gray brute finished his dinner, which took all of twenty seconds, Tom would secure him back in the crate and prepare my breakfast or dinner. By the time Tom ushered me back into the room, the gray brute was sound asleep. *What a loser! Obviously he has never experienced the finer things in life.* We followed this routine for several days.

Although my right front leg was still very sensitive, I was beginning to feel stronger. The area of my gums around where I had lost my canine and adjoining tooth was almost healed. I no longer had to shift food from right to left in order to chew, and while picking up food without two of my teeth was difficult, it really wasn't a nuisance.

Only one part of my healing process was not progressing—my memory. *For the life of me, I can't remember anything after the violent collision. I remember the impact, and then seeing a bright light before I completely blacked out.*

*****

I was adapting as best I could to the confined routine. However, I knew in my heart that I deserved better than this place.

One day, Tom came through the door, accompanied by a different woman. He gestured in my direction and said, "That girl has been through a lot. We think she was probably struck on the right side by a car or truck. She's lucky to be alive."

The woman listened to him and then moved toward me. A sweet scent emanated from her body, and I detected a slight hint of bacon. Her fingers came through the bars on my door and offered me a lovely bacon flavored treat, which I readily took from her hand. Then the woman stood back up and said, "Poor baby. We're going to get someone real nice to adopt you."

The word "adopt" startled me. *Why do I need to be adopted? I already have a life as a princess, or some royalty anyway. I just can't remember what I am or where I came from.*

Tom then pointed over to the gray brute and commented, "The big fella looks like a handful—it's his large size— he's really pretty harmless."

The lady went over and gave the gray brute a treat as well. Predictably, he became so excited that his entire crate gyrated.

He is so plebian, it's unbelievable. Look at him; he can't even control himself enough to get a treat without causing a major disturbance. How ill-mannered!

What astonished me was that instead of being insulted by the gray brute's inappropriate behavior, the lady laughed out loud and said, "He is nothing but a big lovable goofball! He won't be hard to place."

Well, she's right about the goofball part. I cannot vouch for the lovable part. The only time we were in the same room together, he nearly knocked me out!

The lady continued, "The Weimaraner rescue group is sending a couple in this afternoon to meet both dogs. They've completed the paperwork and have passed our initial inspection, so they're qualified to adopt." She looked at me and then at the gray brute, "The group assigned them the names Mila and Augustus on their website."

I froze when I heard this comment. *The gray brute had better be the one called Augustus. Mila does not thrill me as a name, but it does have a certain regal quality to it. However, I'm sure I already possess a perfect name—one suitable to my princess status. If only I could remember it!*

*****

Later that afternoon, Tom came in and walked over to me. "Okay, Mila, you're first. Come with me." Tom opened my door and slid a temporary collar around my neck and attached a leash to it. As we walked through the adjoining room towards the door that led to the lobby of the office, he said to me, "Let's shine," girl. It's show time!"

How embarrassing to be paraded around like a common dog—like that Augustus!

When we came into the lobby, I saw the woman with the bacon-flavored treats standing in the reception area with a man and a woman. As we approached the three of them, the woman with the bacon flavored treats said to me, "Here, Mila," and handed me one of her treats. It had a different flavor than this morning's treat, but was still very tasty. She said, "Folks, this is Mila. She is underweight and has apparently been hit by a car or something. Not only is her leg injured but she lost her right canine tooth and the one next to it." She leaned over me and lifted my lip slightly to show the space that my two teeth used to occupy. When she removed her hand, my lip lodged into the toothless gap.

The man said, "Oh wow, she has a mean little sneer on her face. She kind of resembles Snidely Whiplash." Both the woman with the bacon treats and the other woman laughed out loud.

I don't know who this Snidely Whiplash is but I think I've just been insulted.

The other woman, who smelled like oranges and slightly

musky, as if she'd been gardening, then reached over and gently slid my lip out of the gap so that it hung properly. She said, "There, now you're the beautiful girl that you deserve to be."

I liked her smell and the tone of her voice. *Finally, someone recognizes that I am indeed pretty and special!*

The woman with the bacon treat said, "Why don't you guys interact with Mila a little bit? Feel free to take her out in the yard on a leash. Just be gentle with her because of her leg."

The man said, eagerly, "I'll take her out on a leash. Boy, it's been a long time since I walked a dog."

Oh great, the old rookie wants to be the first to take me on a walk.

As he leaned down to pet my head, I could smell wine and roasted chicken on his breath. I was very familiar with both smells. I love the smell of roasted chicken, but dislike the smell of alcohol. Somehow, my memory of alcohol was very clear. *This particular smell is a very nice wine. Somewhere in my past, I must have become a connoisseur of fine wine. Most wine sommeliers would kill for my sense of smell. However, I still cannot remember why I was so gifted?*

The man and I exited the door to the small fenced-in yard and walked up and back. He looked down at me and said, "What do you think, PJ, do you think you would like to come home with us?"

I did not respond. I thought, *What a knucklehead!* While I couldn't remember my real name, the nice woman with bacon treats referred to me as Mila. It was then that I noticed that he had several paint spots on his old faded blue jeans. *He cannot even afford to dress properly. I can only imagine what his home must look like. This pauper wants to "adopt" me? Really? This man is a complete contradiction! He obviously knows and drinks fine wine but dresses like....well like someone who would adopt the gray brute for instance.* We went back inside.

The woman who smelled like oranges and the garden asked, "How did you two get along?"

The man responded, "I think PJ's a keeper!"

What an imbecile. Did the woman with the bacon not say that my new name is Mila? The woman smiled at the man. *She must really like this man to put up with such ignorance.*

The woman with the bacon treats asked, "Do you not want to see the male?"

The man replied, "Sure. Why not?"

Of course he does. He's a complete moron!

The woman with the bacon treats said, "I have to warn you, Augustus is a really big boy. I don't think he knows his own strength, which is typical of most male Weimaraners. He is just a big lovable goofball."

There she goes again with that "lovable goofball" nonsense. I concur he is "goofball," but I see absolutely nothing loveable about him.

The woman with the bacon treats continued, "On the other hand, females like Mila can be very manipulative."

I can't believe my ears! Up until this point, I thought the lady with bacon was nice...maybe a little misguided but still nice. What is this manipulative business? I am not manipulative at all. I just have high expectations, as would anyone who has shared my social status.

Tom grabbed my leash and took me back to my space. The gray brute was gyrating uncontrollably in his crate when he saw Tom and me enter the room. Tom took me off the leash and motioned for me to enter my crate. I gladly complied and circled my space a few times before lying down so I could have a good view of the room. I did not want to miss the spectacle that was about to unfold once the gray brute was released from his space. He, of course, assumed he was just going outside to stretch his legs and take care of some business. I could tell when all the commotion erupted in the next room, the precise moment when he discovered that he was going to the reception area and not the yard.

He's going to make quite an impression on the couple—but not a good one. He will probably blindside both of them and knock them down like bowling pins. On the other hand, the man doesn't seem too bright. They might just be perfectly suited for each other.

Although I was two rooms away, I could still hear the commotion in the lobby. One of the ladies yelled, "Be careful, don't knock over the chair!" When it quieted down, I decided to close my eyes and get a quick nap and take advantage of the opportunity to finally be alone. My repose didn't last long. A few minutes later, I woke to the familiar and disgusting panting. Tom walked the gray brute over to his crate, motioned for him to enter, and secured the door behind him. Then Tom turned his head in my direction and said, "Sorry to bother you, girl, but they want to see you again."

Really? They want me to parade before them again? This type of treatment is so beneath me. I am not some circus animal that performs for peanuts. While I still cannot remember, I am absolutely positive that I had people wait on me and cater to my every whim.

Tom opened the door to my space and did not bother to attach a leash to my temporary collar. He said, "I know you don't need a leash to behave. I can tell you were taken care of in your prior world."

Tom seems to be the only person in this place that has a clue of my prestigious background.

I reluctantly followed Tom back into the reception area. The man and woman were standing there visiting with the woman with the bacon treats. They did not look too worse for wear. Judging from the earlier disturbance, I had assumed that someone had gotten hurt after their encounter with the gray brute. The man kneeled down as I approached with Tom. He clicked twice with his mouth for some apparent reason and motioned with his hand for me to come to him. Instead, I caught a whiff of something fascinating just to my right. Instead of walking over to the man, I followed a wonderful scent to my right, which was emanating from a trashcan under the receptionist's desk.

I heard the lady with the bacon treat ask, "Where's she going?"

Tom had not seen me slip off on my investigation behind his back and responded, "I don't know. I'll find out." When Tom found me, my head was completely submerged in a trashcan. I had discovered quite a treasure. Someone had discarded almost a quarter of a ham sandwich concealed in a brown paper bag. *Who would throw away good food like this?* Tom grabbed me by my temporary collar, pulled my head out of the trashcan, and said rather sternly, "Girl, you know you're not that hungry!"

While I liked Tom, he obviously did not understand that you never pass up an opportunity when food is involved, whether you are particularly hungry or not. He pointed towards the front of the reception area and gave me a slight push. I shot him a quick glance. *I got it! I am going up to where the couple is standing right now!*

When I approached the couple, the woman with the bacon treat said, "I think you made a good choice." She and the other woman went over to the counter and began filling out some paperwork. The man slipped a leash onto my temporary collar and walked me over to one of the reception area chairs. I obediently sat next to him.

The woman with the bacon treat said to the man, "I think she will adapt nicely to whatever name you want to call her."

I sighed. *So, why don't you call me by my real name? I just don't remember what it is.*

The man responded to the woman with the bacon treat, "Thanks, Jenni!" he stared down at me. "Your name will be Polly Jean. However, we're going to call you PJ for short. Are you okay with that?" He leaned down to rub behind my ears.

While I somewhat appreciated the attention, I would have preferred some of the roasted chicken that I could again smell on his breath. I guess he must have touched his pants while he was eating, because I could detect a slight roasted chicken scent on his jeans. As I turned to get a closer sniff, I again noticed the paint splatters.

I really think this guy should've chosen the gray brute. They seem a better fit.

He rubbed my head again and leaned down and whispered in my ear; "I promise you, girlfriend, you will never be hungry or get hurt again!"

That's quite a promise for a guy wearing paint-splattered blue jeans. You will have to convince me.

The woman with the bacon treats and the other woman walked over to the man and me. The woman with the orange and garden scent said to the man, "You might want to read this over. It's the terms and conditions of the adoption. We have up to a week to change our minds if this girl turns out to be incompatible with us."

"Thanks," he said. "I'll read it thoroughly when I get home."

Don't I get a say in this? Aren't I a party to this contract?

The man stood and said to the woman with the bacon treats, "Thanks for all you have done, Jenni. I think PJ is going to be very happy with us."

The woman with bacon treats smiled, "I am sure she'll be very happy. Please don't hesitate to contact me if you have any questions, or if, for whatever reason, she doesn't work out." The two women hugged.

The man looked down at me and said, "This will probably be your first ride in a Mini Cooper. I apologize for the small amount of room, PJ, but I promise you one thing—you will love your new backyard."

This guy makes a lot of promises.

3

Green Space and Blue Water

I jumped into the back of the car and attempted to avoid landing on my sore leg. A few minutes into the ride, I understood why the man apologized. The car trunk/ backseat was cramped with uneven surfaces. *Surely I had better accommodations in my prior life.* I tried to lie down and relax. However, every time I almost got comfortable, the man would make a turn, causing me to slide back and forth. I had all the grace of the gray brute.

After what seemed like an eternity, the man turned down an alley covered with mature trees. He had left the two backseat windows cracked open. I could smell a variety of aromas. The man did something with his hand, which seemed to trigger the movement of an enormous wooden gate along a track. When he was satisfied that the opening was large enough, the man eased his car through it to a large concrete landing. No sooner had he cleared the opening, then the gate began to close behind us. The man pulled his car into the garage and turned off the engine. I became a little restless, having traveled so far in this cramped space. The man and the woman got out of the car and closed both front doors. I was afraid the man and woman would forget and leave me in the car. *How do I get out of here?* I noticed some straps that extended from the roof of the car to the front seat. The woman and man had both buckled these straps around their shoulders before initially starting the car. *Is it possible that the straps might have something to do with opening the door or trunk of the car?* As is my nature, I immediately focused on the task at hand. I walked over to the strap the woman had used and began to gnaw on it with the left side of my mouth. About the time that I was starting to make some progress in unraveling the threads on the strap, the trunk of the car popped open. *That is easier than I thought.* I had assumed that I would have to sever both straps in order to gain my freedom.

The man peered into the car from outside the trunk. He shouted in my direction, "What do you think you're doing in there? Don't chew my seatbelts!" I could tell by the inflection in his voice that he disapproved of my actions to free myself from the Mini Cooper. He continued now in a quieter and kinder voice, "I'm sorry. I didn't mean to yell at you. But, you cannot chew up my car. You were unattended for only a moments. I wanted to open the gate to the yard so it would be the first thing you saw when you got to your new home. Come on, jump out and check out your new backyard."

I followed the man's instructions and gingerly crawled out of the trunk and safely landed on the concrete of the garage floor. The man motioned me to follow him out of the garage and through a gate that led to a beautiful green space. I could not believe my eyes! I saw grass, trees, and a pond. I became so mesmerized that I completely forgot where I was. I sprinted as fast I could to the other side of the green space mindful not to put any undue pressure on my injured leg. There were so many pleasant and strange odors to investigate. I could smell a squirrel here, a rabbit here. *Wow, this is a really special place.*

Several minute had passed before I thought to check on the man to make sure he had not abandoned me or done something else foolish. He was still there, leaning on the fence next to the gate with a silly grin on his face. *Why is he grinning at me? I felt a little embarrassed and hung my head and turned away.*

He called out to me, "PJ, what do you think of your new backyard?"

I decided to ignore him and continue to sniff around and get the lay of the land. This green space or, "backyard," as the man referred to it was configured into two intersecting rectangles. It appeared to be surrounded by giant bushes. There was a nice blue pond on one of the rectangles and a building bordered one side of the backyard. Yes, *this is quite a place. I could spend hours exploring out here.*

After a few more minutes of investigation, I decided that I should again check on the man. When I looked back towards the gate, he was no longer in sight. A sudden panic set in. *Did he leave me here all alone?* I sprinted back to the gate and noticed that it was shut. I riveted my head around, trying to get a glimpse of the man, but he was definitely not there. *What am I going to do? I don't think I can hurdle this fence with my sore leg. There must be a way out of this place somewhere.* I decided to check the perimeter of the backyard. I trotted over to the enormous bushes. As I got closer, I could make out a wood fence just beyond where they stood. I maneuvered my body through a gap in one of the bushes so that I was standing in a narrow space just between the bushes and the fence.

When I surveyed the area, I could tell that I was not the first creature to have come to this place. In fact, there was a path that led between the bushes and the fence for the entire periphery. When I sniffed a bit, I picked up several scents. There was even a faint scent of a dog. *I wonder if he or she is still somewhere near.* I decided to walk the entire trail to see if there were obvious escape routes. It all looked pretty secure. There were a few places that I could see that someone had dug a small opening under the fence. It was way too small for a dog. I suspected it was probably a pesky squirrel or some other vermin. While I couldn't remember any specifics of my life prior to my accident, I did know that I did not care for squirrels. They seem to serve no purpose in life other than to interrupt my naps with their annoying chattering.

When I reached the end of the trail, I came to an opening. The bushes stopped just short of an intersecting connecting fence. One end of the fence attached to the fence with the bushes and the other end to the building structure. There was also a huge gate. I noticed that there were a few gaps between the gate and the fence where, if I held my head just right, I could see through to the other side. However, the gaps were not large enough for me to slip through. I peeked through and saw more green space and a street. There was no time to speculate on what was there; I was on a mission to find an escape route. I continued to follow the fence to the building structure. I sniffed around the building. There were all kinds of scents present. I continued sniffing around the building structure until I rounded the corner and eventually came upon a wooden deck. I thought, *this would be a nice place to sun if I were not determined to escape.*

My thoughts were interrupted by the sound of a door opening. I then noticed that two doors led out onto the deck from the building. The man was standing in the entryway of one of the doors. He said, "Are you getting acquainted with your backyard?

Where have you been? In another few minutes, I would have figured out an opening where I could've escaped to freedom!

He then said, "Are you thirsty? I've filled up this new

water bowl full of fresh water." He was gesturing at a stainless steel bowl, which had been placed carefully so that it would always be in the shade.

I walked over and sniffed the bowl of water but did not take a drink from it. I thought, *why would I drink water out of this bowl when there is a nice blue pond a mere few steps away with what I can only imagine is very fresh water?* To further emphasize my point, I turned around and walked out to the blue pond and began lapping up water from the shallow end. I could smell and taste some chemical, but it was not unpleasant. It certainly tasted better than some water, which I am sure I'd had to drink before my accident.

The man shouted at me, "Hey, you're not supposed to drink out of my swimming pool!" I could tell by the tone of his voice that he was not angry. To the contrary, he seemed rather amused at my self-sufficiency. He walked out to where I was standing and pulled something from his pocket. As he drew nearer, I could smell a slight odor of beef. The man asked, "Would you care for a little jerky treat?"

I performed a cautionary investigation with my nose to make sure this wasn't a trick. I reached over and took the treat from the man. *I had better in the past I am sure. But, it was not too bad.*

I heard another door that led onto the deck open. When I glanced up from the crumbs of my former treat, I saw the woman walking on the deck toward the man and me. She held some round object in her hand. She handed it discreetly to the man and said, "Be careful! Remember her hurt leg."

The man laughed and responded, "I understand. I just want her to know what fun awaits her when she's completely healed." He took the round object and extended his hand in my direction. I took a quick sniff and could tell that it clearly was not food. I turned to walk away when I heard the man ask, "Don't tell me you don't like tennis balls? Every dog loves to play ball."

The woman said, "Maybe she's just too hurt to be interested. She obviously has been through a lot."

I am not sure about the man, but I think the woman has potential. She seems to have insight that he is clearly lacking.

The man was persistent. He walked passed me into the middle of the green space next to the pond. The woman and I just stood and stared at him. The man extended the round object behind his back and then quickly brought his arm forward. While his arm was in the forward position, he released the round object and it went sailing to the other side of the green space. He seemed pleased with this result. He shouted in our general direction. "PJ is going to love the distance she can travel to retrieve tennis balls." The man took off running towards where the round object laid on the grass. He then proceeded to pick it up and turned his body to face the direction from where he had just come. Using the same maneuver with his arm, the round object again sailed through the air and landed approximately where the man had previously stood. Once again, the man began running in the direction where the ball had landed.

The woman and I watched in silence. The man repeated his actions several times. I could hear him breathing heavily from all this exercise. The woman finally said, "Well, I don't know about PJ, but you certainly seem to enjoy pitching and fetching the tennis ball."

Both the man and woman laughed, then began talking amongst themselves. I was bored so I sauntered over next to the blue pond and found a nice spot in the sun to lie down. Every once in a while, I would glance over towards the man and woman to make sure they did not abandon me.

4

Furniture Rules

I was out of earshot and could not hear what they were discussing. But, it did not seem to pertain to me since they were not looking in my direction. Finally, the man looked over at me and whistled.

I did not move a muscle. *Why did he suddenly whistle at me? Is a whistle supposed to elicit some kind of response from me?* I groaned, but otherwise remained still. I could sense that the man was becoming frustrated about something judging by his body language.

He then shouted in my direction, "PJ, don't you understand when I whistle you are supposed to come to me?"

I did not move.

The woman shouted, "PJ, come check out your new

home!" She had a sweetness and kindness to her voice even when shouting. I rose to my feet and walked over to where the man and woman were standing. She reached down and patted my head. "Good girl! Now, let's go inside."

I followed the woman and the man brought up the rear. We walked into a room that had hardwood floors and a rug positioned directly in the center of the room. There were three chairs, but none of them looked like they would offer a comfortable place for me to take a nap. I followed the woman into another adjoining room. It had a nice looking sofa and three chairs. The sofa looked like a potential sleeping spot. The woman sat on the sofa and the man in one of the chairs. They began to talk about everything except me. It had been about seven hours since Tom prepared my breakfast. It was late in the afternoon and I could feel hunger pangs creeping in. *If they are going to ignore me, then I might as well get comfortable.* I walked over to an unoccupied part of the sofa and effortlessly leapt upon it. No sooner had I landed then I became the center of everyone's attention.

Both the man and woman let out a collective, "No!!!" The man shouted, "Get down! No paws on the furniture!" I was completely blindsided by this unusual and rude behavior, but I obeyed. I step slowly off the sofa.

The woman then said softly, "Don't yell at her. She didn't know it was wrong to get on the sofa." She scooted down the sofa until she was next to where I stood and started rubbing my head. "You didn't know you were doing anything wrong, did you, sweet girl?"

Finally, some sanity is restored. I lay down at the woman's feet and turned over to expose my belly to her. She got down on the floor with me and began to softly rub my belly.

The man said, "Well, she has certainly found the soft spot hasn't she?" The man rose from his chair and walked into the next room. I could tell he was doing something of interest because I was familiar with this sound. I sprung to my feet and trotted to where the man had gone, leaving the woman on the ground behind me. I heard the man shout to the woman, "I thought she might be hungry!" He began scooping out some beef smelling pellets into a stainless steel bowl. When he was finished, he held the bowl over my head and said, "PJ, are you hungry?

Of course, I'm hungry! How can you be so obtuse?

The man then repeated himself, except with a little more animation, "I said, 'PJ, are you hungry?'"

I could not figure out what kind of response the man was trying to elicit from me. So I improvised. I decided to remain perfectly still and stare at him eye to eye with the same disapproving stare that I had given the gray brute. *What will this man do next?* I wondered.

The man screamed "PJ, I asked if you were hungry!" The inflection in his voice was very different from when he shouted at me earlier when I decided to join the woman on the sofa.

No, he's not angry. He's trying to play some sort of a game. Well, I must go to Plan B—my best gray brute impersonation. Without warning, I leapt up and knocked the bowl of food cleanly out of the man's hand.

By his reaction, he was obviously surprised by my tactic. The bowl came crashing down on the hardwood floor and clanged loudly. All the contents from the bowl were scattered all over the floor. The man began laughing out loud and said, "I guess I have my answer."

Time was of the essence. I began hurriedly eating every beef pellet off the floor that I could locate.

I heard the woman shout from the next room, "What's going on in there?"

The man shouted back, "PJ and I were just having a conversation. I wanted to make certain that she was hungry and she certainly convinced me that she indeed was hungry."

By the time the woman arrived from the next room, I had successfully located and consumed every one of the beef pellets on the floor. I decided to give the floor a few gratuitous licks for good measure.

After eating up the pellets, the man and I went outside. I pretty much followed my last routine where I would investigate a bit while periodically keeping an eye on him. I was not going to let him out of my sight for more than a few seconds at a time. After I found the perfect spot to take care of some business, the man and I re-entered the house. This time, the couple settled into a different room. They sat side by side. In front of them was a bluish flat screen that contain a lot of people's voices. I decided to locate a comfortable place on the floor next to an unoccupied chair. At first, I thought about hopping up into it, but it did not appear comfortable to me. After about an hour of staring at the bluish screen, the woman got out of her chair and disappeared into an adjoining room.

It was the same room where I'd knocked the bowl of beef pellets out of the man's hand earlier. Within a few minutes, I could smell a wonderful aroma. *This is worth investigating.* I rose to my feet and wandered into the adjoining room. A fleeting recollection came to me—*a kitchen.*

The woman stood next to a counter. She was stirring something in a pot. I could not make out the scent, but I knew it must be delicious. She looked down at me and smiled. "Our last dog loved parmesan cheese. Would you like to try a piece?" She gently extended her hand down to a few inches above my nose. Before she could change her mind, I quickly snatched the cheese cleanly out of her hand. My sudden and somewhat aggressive response startled her a bit. She recoiled and said, "Easy girl! Just the cheese and not my fingers!"

The woman then shouted to the man in the other room, "When would you like to eat dinner?" There was a slight pause and I heard the man respond, "How about thirty minutes from now? I want to take a few minutes to read PJ's adoption agreement."

The woman said, "That's fine. Just give me a few minutes notice so I can pull everything together." The woman walked back into the room where the man was sitting and sat in a chair beside him. Since there was no longer any food being offered to me, I decided to follow the woman and lay down on the floor next to where she was sitting. The man began to read aloud, "It appears in the first paragraph that we have agreed to provide PJ with free run of the house, fresh water, wholesome food, adequate outdoor exercise, and affection." He stopped reading momentarily and took a drink of wine, which rested on a table next to him. *I enjoyed the taste of wine but the initial scent of alcohol always deterred me from drinking it. Yes, I remember a large house with a huge man. He always had a glass of wine in his private area. I would curl up next to him on the couch. When he would pretend to offer me a drink from his glass, I would turn my head. This always struck him as terribly funny.* The man began reading again, "It says here in the second paragraph that we agree never to use the dog for dog fighting or any other activity where the dog is pitted against another dog." He stopped reading and began to snicker.

The woman asked, "What's so funny?"

He responded, "Well since PJ is missing her canine tooth, I doubt she'll be engaging in any fighting." The woman and man both laughed.

They may make fun of me, but I assure you that I can take of myself. I don't remember how long, but I must have been on the streets for a while before my accident.

The man then remarked, "I wonder if there is any provision in this agreement concerning her sneering like Snidely Whiplash?" The woman and man both laughed out loud again.

Really....you consider the fact that I lost my canine tooth funny?

The man said, "Here is the provision that Jenni referenced about having a five-day trial period to see if we are compatible." He set the agreement on the table next to his wine glass and said, "I probably should have read this agreement before we signed it. You'd think as an attorney I would have known better." The man chuckled to himself and ran a hand over his bald head. He looked down at me and asked, "We all have a five-day grace period to revoke the agreement. Do you think we will need it, sweet girl?"

Finally, he is treating me with some modicum of respect, which I deserve.

Instead of reacting to his question I rolled over onto my left side and let out a slight groan. The man commented, "I'll take a groan as your response—whatever that means."

The man stood up with the agreement in one hand and his wine glass in the other and asked, "Are you ready for dinner now?"

The woman stood up and responded, "Sure! Just give me ten minutes to get it ready."

The man disappeared into another part of the house for a few minutes and then returned with only his wine glass. He joined the woman in what I would soon learn was the dining room. Like the kitchen, it held wonderful smells of food. The woman said, "Do you think it is safe to eat in front of PJ?"

There was a pause before the man replied, "Just to be on the safe side I am going to put her behind that indoor dog fence that I purchased yesterday."

I watched as the man left the room and walked into another part of the house. He soon returned with some kind of metal contraption that was folded together. He started to unfold it and then stopped. "I'd better get a treat to get PJ on the other side before I assemble the fence." The man walked over to a cabinet and ripped open a plastic bag. I immediately smelled the wonderful scent of bacon. He resealed the bag and returned it to the cabinet. I could tell that he had something in his hand. He walked over to me and waved his bacon flavored right hand just above my head. "Come on, girl, follow me!"

I knew to always follow the food if it was an option. Keeping an eye securely focused on his right hand, I followed the man into the next room. When we were just beyond the doorway that led to the next room, the man handed me the bacon flavored treat from his right hand. "PJ this is your reward for staying on this side of the fence while we eat dinner." The man then took a step back and continued to unfold the metal contraption he referred to as a fence. After struggling for a few minutes, he successfully attached each side of the fence within the doorway, which separated the kitchen from the room where I stood. I watched as he tested it by applying pressure and shaking it. Apparently satisfied with his work, the man said, "This should hold her. It's pretty secure. Besides, with her hurt front leg, she shouldn't have a lot of strength."

The man walked back into the dining room and left me alone in the dark room.

I should investigate this fence that separates me from the room with its lovely smells. I sniffed the entire perimeter of the barrier. From the noise in the other part of the house, I could tell that the man and woman were eating their dinner. *Why would they exclude me from dinner? Don't we have an agreement? I just heard the man read from the agreement, "we have agreed to provide PJ with free run of the house, fresh water, and wholesome food!" We haven't been together a full day and the man has already breached our contract. I should have free run of the house and wholesome food. While the beef pellets were a nice appetizer, I'm sure from the aromas that the man and woman are eating something much more delicious. I'm sure this whole barrier thing was the man's idea. The woman is so much kinder and gentler than he is with me. I know people pretty well.*

I began testing the sturdiness of the fence. I gave it a good nudge with my head. It moved slightly each time that I pushed it in the middle with my head. *This is doable! I just need some leverage.* I pushed on the lowest part, but it did not budge. Thwarted by the lower portion, I decided to go high and try to apply some force. I took a few steps backwards and stared at the fence to determine the best spot to target. Without any more hesitation, I ran and leapt, striking it dead center at the top perimeter. Much to my delight, the fence came crashing down and fell into the kitchen. *That wasn't too difficult.*

I step over the fallen gate and walked into the kitchen where I was met by the man. He had a napkin in his left hand and a glass of wine in his right hand.

This guy drinks a lot of wine, I thought.

He gave me a stern look and asked rather rudely, "PJ, what do you think you're doing?"

Trying to uphold my end of the agreement by having free run of the house and enjoying wholesome food. Remember paragraph one of our agreement?

He walked over to where the fence lay bent out of shape and crumpled on the floor. He yelled at me, "PJ, I think you broke the damn thing! How could a malnourished dog with a hurt front leg possibly apply enough pressure to knock this fence down?"

The woman had now joined us in the kitchen. She said in a soft tone, "Look, I think you scared her." The woman walked over to me and patted me on the head. "You didn't mean to do anything wrong, did you, girlfriend?"

She seems to understand the agreement. I'm not sure what his problem is though.

The woman's demeanor relieved the tense situation and she steered him back into the dining room. They sat down at the table and finished eating their dinner. I decided to lie down in the doorway that separated the kitchen from the dining room. I tried to look like I was sleeping, but I kept an eye on them.

The man and woman ate in silence for a few minutes. Finally, the woman said, "Look how cute she is lying there between the kitchen and the dining room."

The man responded, "She definitely likes to keep one of us in sight at all times."

When the man and woman finished their dinner, they both got up from the table with their plates in hand. Both of them had to step over me to enter the kitchen. The man turned on the faucet to let the water heat up. He called over to me, "PJ, I have a tradition with all my dogs that I think might be of interest to you."

I stood up to get a better look at the man. *He had something in his hand that had a nice aroma.*

He extended his hand in my general direction and said, "Girlfriend, I always save something from my meals for the dog of the house. That is you now, girl...assuming neither one of us voids our agreement within the next five days." He laughed out loud after he finished his sentence.

I promptly approached his hand and gave it a slight sniff. I wasn't certain exactly what it was, but it smelled wonderful and I knew that it must be tasty. Cautiously, I removed the morsel of food from the man's hand. *I don't understand this man. One minute he is yelling at me and the next he's giving me a lovely treat.* The man then turned around and began rinsing the dishes off in the sink. *While I appreciate the treat, I would have also enjoyed licking your plate.*

5

Guests for the Evening

It was my first day with the man and woman. I suppose they were excited and honored to have me in their home because they invited some guests over to meet me. The man went out into the backyard and walked over to the pond. I watched him through the glass window of the door that led onto a wooden deck and eventually out to the pond.

If I ever get stranded outside at least I have a good source of water.

The man picked up a net attached to a long pole and started skimming it over the surface of the pond. I had no idea what he was doing, but he seemed content enough. I heard the woman in the kitchen, so I thought I would join her. She was busy assembling some food items on to trays

---

that rested on the counter. One item, in particular, caught my attention. I knew instantly that it was brie cheese as soon as she removed it from the refrigerator. Even though it was wrapped in plastic, I could smell its lovely aroma.

This is like my knowledge of fine wine. Somehow, somewhere in my past, I was also a connoisseur of fine cheeses. There are many fine cheeses out there, but brie is special. It pairs well with many wines. I wonder if the man and woman will be serving their guests a lovely wine tonight. On the other hand, the woman may have selected the brie for me. After all, she has been nothing but kind and gentle to me since we entered into our agreement early today.

The woman placed some crackers on the tray next to the plastic encased brie. She then left the kitchen. I followed her. She walked through the den and down a hallway to a large bedroom. I knew it was a bedroom from the bedding and pillows. *I recall sleeping on something very similar to this bed before.* I was a few steps behind her. She walked through the room and entered another small room that was attached and shut the door behind her.

Should I attempt to open the door and follow her?

I glanced to my right through the glass door that led onto the deck from the bedroom, and saw the man still skimming the pond with a net. Instead of attempting to follow the woman, I decided to retrace my footsteps. When I walked back into the den I noticed that the door that led to the deck was left slightly ajar. The night was cool and the man must not have been concerned with making sure the door was completely shut. I trotted into the kitchen. The brie cheese and crackers were still there on the counter. I reared up and landed my two front paws squarely onto the counter. The brie cheese still wrapped in plastic smelled heavenly. With the precision of a skilled surgeon, I leaned over and grabbed the entire block of cheese with the left side of my mouth careful not to disturb the crackers on the plate. Gently, I eased my front paws off the counter and landed with a slight thud on the kitchen floor. I glanced around with the plastic-wrapped block of cheese securely clinched in my mouth to see if my actions had been detected. No one was around.

I walked back into the den and peered out the glass door. The man was still skimming the pond with the net. I walked over and nudged the door with my head. The door opened just wide enough for me to squeeze through before shutting behind me. Fortunately, the man did not hear the door open and close because he did not turn around. I trotted over to a nice comfortable place in the grass and lay down. *Now it is time to savor this wonderful brie cheese.* I bit off a nice healthy chunk and quickly consumed it along with the plastic wrapper. When I was about three quarters through eating the entire block, I heard the woman shout from the deck to the man, "Did you do something with the cheese?"

He set down his net and turned to face the woman and shouted back, "What cheese?"

The woman had a puzzled look on her face. She took a

few steps forward on the deck so that she would not have to shout so loud. "So, you didn't take the cheese off the counter?"

The man also walked closer to the woman. "No. I didn't know that we had any cheese."

During this exchange of conversation, I continued to stare first at the woman then at the man. The remainder of the brie was resting safely underneath my two front paws. The woman then looked over in my direction. She started walking towards me and shouted, "PJ, did you steal the cheese off the counter?"

The man was following closely behind her. As they approached me, he shouted, "Why, that little thief!" Mere seconds later, the man and woman were standing directly in front of me and my prized brie.

The woman reached towards the cheese but before she could grasp it, I bit down hard on the remaining block and then whipped my head to the right to avoid contact.

The man screamed, "PJ, drop it!"

Instead of dropping the cheese I tightened my clinch on it.

The woman then gently said to me, "PJ, that cheese was for our guests tonight. You're a naughty girl!"

It was not so much what she said, but the manner in which she said it that caused me to release my grip. The remaining cheese and teeth punctured plastic came tumbling out of my mouth in a single lump. It bounced and landed squarely on top of the man's right shoe. He reached down and removed the cheese from his shoe and groaned, "This is ruined! What she didn't eat has her slobber or teeth marks on it. Look, she ate it with the plastic still on it."

The woman responded, "The plastic should do wonders for her digestive system."

The man and woman turned around and began walking towards the deck. I followed closely behind thinking, *The brie is not ruined. I am more than happy to take it off your hands.* The three of us reentered the house and walked through the den back into the kitchen. The man walked over to a fancy trashcan, pressed down a lever with his foot, causing the lid to pop open, and deposited the cheese block into the open can. He removed his foot, and the lid snapped shut.

I can't believe he just threw away perfectly good brie! He must not be too bright! He claims to be an attorney, yet he doesn't understand contracts. This is absurd! He agreed to provide me with wholesome food. What could be more wholesome than brie cheese?

A few minutes passed, and I heard a bell ring from the hallway. Immediately, both the man and the woman walked passed me. I decided to follow them. They continued through the front room of the house and paused a moment at the door that led outside to the front of the house. The woman swung open the door and another woman and a man came inside the house. The men shook hands and the women hugged. No one noticed that I had drawn nearer.

While the women hugged, I circled around so that I was standing behind the visiting woman. *I'm picking up a scent but cannot identify the source.* I leaned forward and placed my nose directly on her rear end. I smelled something delicious emanating from a small covered tray that the visiting woman held in her hand. Apparently, the sensation of my nose making contact with her rear end caused her to flinch and take a step forward. She stumbled and temporarily lost her balance. This reaction caused her to drop her covered tray. It went crashing to the hardwood floor. The cover flew off of the tray, revealing some lovely smelling cookies. She said, "Oh my god, your dog just goosed me!"

The words were no sooner out of her mouth, then I had made my way around her over to where the tray lay on the floor. Without stopping to take an initial sniff, I grabbed the nearest cookie from the tray. My actions did not go unnoticed. The man shouted, "PJ, no!" He motioned for me to move out of the way. I thought, *He sure does shout a lot!* He then knelt down and picked up the tray and cover from off the floor. He said, "So sorry about this! PJ obviously needs to work on her manners. Earlier tonight, we discovered that she's also a cheese thief. She helped herself to a nice block of brie that we intended to serve to you guys tonight."

The visiting woman responded, "That's okay, PJ, no harm done."

She sounds as nice as the woman of the house. Why can't the man be as considerate?

For the remainder of the night, the people talked, drank wine, and nibbled on food. Most of the time, they just stood in the kitchen, which suited me just fine. Occasionally, one or another of them would accidentally drop some crumbs on the floor. Each time that happened I made a mental note. From my position of lying quietly on the floor, I could casually observe all the action. I suspected that if I had immediately walked over to check out these crumbs each time they fell to the floor, the man would have yelled at me again. Quite frankly, I was tired and I'd had enough excitement for one night.

Finally, everyone except me walked out of the kitchen and to the front door. As soon as they exited the kitchen, I leapt to my feet and went over to claim my treasured crumbs. There were a combination of the visiting woman's cookies and some salty tasting crackers. I thought, *the crackers, in particular, would have gone well with the block of brie that I only partially consumed earlier this evening. I still cannot fathom why the man thought it was necessary to throw away perfectly good brie just because of a little drool and teeth punctures. He's certainly a strange one. If my contract was just with him, I think I would void it tomorrow after breakfast. The woman, on the other hand, is gentle and really seems to understand me. I think she and I will continue to get along nicely.*

I was getting tired and decided to find a comfortable place to sleep. I was with the couple in their den. They were staring at the blue screen. When I got up from the floor, the man said, "Are you ready to go to sleep, PJ? You've had a full day—with the adoption, you getting accustomed to your new home, and meeting new people, you must be exhausted.

I froze in my tracks and stared up at him as he spoke.

"Come on, girl, you have a wonderful bed back here in this media room.

The man led me to the same room that he'd put me in before they'd had their dinner. Instead of putting a barrier between the two of us, he led me over to the corner where a blanket had been placed on top of a cushion.

He said, "PJ, this is where you are going to sleep tonight. I promise to get you a more permanent bed in the next few days. You should be comfortable here, though."

This is not up to the standard accommodations of which, I am almost certain, I was accustomed to in my past. In fact, the bedding in the large bedroom would be perfect for my needs. However, I am sure it will do for the night.

I walked over and stepped on the blanket and spun around three times before settling down. The man quietly watched me until I stopped moving.

"PJ, you seem comfortable enough. I am going to put what is left of this dog fence back in place just for tonight. I want to make sure that you don't decide during the night that our B&B Italia sofa might be a more appropriate choice for your bed."

I listened as he attempted to reinstall the fence in the doorway. The man seemed to be struggling to get it positioned where he wanted it. He whispered, "Girlfriend, you did a number on this doggie fence. Please be a good girl and leave it alone until I come get you in the morning. I promise to be here bright and early." The man switched off the light and walked back into the den.

I thought, *The man is right, I have had a full day.* I closed my eyes, groaned, and fell soundly to sleep.

6

Day Two of the Trial Period

Early the next morning, I opened my eyes. Sunlight was streaming in through the window. I got to my feet and stretched. First my front legs, and then my back ones. While my makeshift bed could have been more comfortable, I did sleep well. *Now, I must go locate the man and woman so they can let me outside to take care of some business.* I walked over and sniffed the fence meant to keep me separated from the rest of the house. I nudged it ever so slightly with my nose. The pressure on its bent frame caused it to gap at the bottom about a foot. *If I get down on my belly, I think I can crawl under the bottom of this thing.* Sure enough, I was able to maneuver my body and squirm to the other side of the fence.

When I started to stand up on the other side, my nub

of a tail just grazed the bottom of the fence, causing the fence to swing back into place. It looked as it did when the man first erected it a few hours ago. There was absolutely no evidence to reveal how I ended up on the other side. I walked through the kitchen and down the long hallway, which led to the bedrooms. I could hear the man snoring behind the closed door. I pushed on the door with my nose, but it did not give. The noise though apparently startled the woman in the next room. I heard her say, "What was that noise?"

The man stopped snoring and responded, "Probably just a squirrel on the roof or something. It can't be PJ because she's behind the doggie fence. Let's go back to sleep."

I waited in anticipation, hoping one of them would open the door and let me in. After all, it was morning and I really wanted to step outside for a while before breakfast. *Time for Plan B.* I shook my ears, which sounded like an amplified deck of cards being shuffled. *This tactic always seemed to get people's attention.* I shook them a second time for good measure. Sure enough, I heard some grumbling on the other side of the door, which was followed by footsteps on the hardwood floor. The door swung open and there stood the man, wearing nothing but a pair of boxer shorts and a t-shirt. He gave me a stern look and said, "PJ, it's 5:30 Sunday morning. Girlfriend, we need our sleep! Did you knock down your doggie fence again?"

I just sat and stared up at him until he finished talking.

Really, knocked it down? Don't you think you would have heard the crash of the metal fence hitting the floor? By now, I really needed to go outside so I stood up and walked down the hallway back through the den and stood next to the glass door that led to the backyard. I could hear the man walking behind me. When the man entered the den, he said, "Okay, PJ, I'll let you outside." He unlocked the door and held it open for me as I trotted across the deck to find a perfect grassy spot to take care of my business. The man waited at the door for me to return. Rather than immediately return, I decided to investigate a smell that was emanating from underneath the wood deck. I was familiar with this smell. *It has to be a rabbit.*

Apparently, my failure to return directly to the back door irritated the man. He hollered in my direction, "PJ, it's early and I want to go back to bed! Besides, don't you want some breakfast?"

Breakfast is a magic word that I learned many years ago, which means "food." I trotted back over to the door and into the den. The man promptly closed and locked the door behind me.

When we reentered the house, I saw that the woman was also awake. She was headed to the kitchen. She said to the man, "Are you hungry...or is it too early to eat breakfast?"

The man responded, "We might as well eat since we're up. But first, I want to check on the doggie fence." They walked into the kitchen and through the small hallway that separated the room where I slept from the kitchen. I decided to follow behind them. The two were obviously perplexed when they saw the fence. The man scratched his bald head and finally said, "How in the world did PJ get on our side of the fence? It's just as I left it last night." He gave it a slight nudge with his hand and it quivered ever so slightly.

The woman said, "Maybe she jumped over it."

The man looked over at me and replied, "I don't think that's possible with her hurt leg. Maybe after her leg heals, but not now."

He folded the metal contraption from each end. "I guess I'll buy a second fence to place over the first one. She might be able to hurdle one...but two? I'll just put this in the garage for now."

By this time, I was getting really hungry for breakfast. I followed the woman into the kitchen and watched as she removed some items from the refrigerator. The man joined in the kitchen and said, "I am going to go get the paper and then I'll feed the girl." I walked to the edge of the kitchen and watched as the man opened the front door and walked out of the house.

Let's see...when the man fed me last night, he poured some meaty nuggets in a stainless steel bowl and then paused before placing it before me. For some reason, he wanted me to impersonate the gray brute and attack him before he would feed me. The man is certainly a strange one. However, if he wants me to attack him for food, then I will certainly oblige. He has breached our agreement several times by prohibiting me from having full access to the house. On the other hand, I like the woman and the man does seem harmless enough. I'm going to do something nice for the man to show my good faith in this whole affair. As soon as he comes back into the kitchen, I'm not going to wait for him to put my breakfast in a bowl before acting like the gray brute on him. Instead, I am going to attack him immediately. That's sure to please him.

There was a click and a thud as the man opened the front door to reenter the house. I'd decided to go and lay down on the carpet in the den. *Sooner or later, the man would have to walk by in order to get to the kitchen. The carpet would provide good traction for my claws when the proper time came to pounce on him.*

I heard the man walking down the hallway towards the den. In preparation for my prey, I was hunkered down low to the ground. The man did not appear to notice my presence. He was too busy reading the newspaper as he slowly made his way to where I was positioned.

Careful now, let's not give him any warning at all. My legs were trembling with excitement and anticipation as I waited for just the right moment to spring. *He's going to be so surprised and pleased with me.*

I let him get just passed me before I leapt in his direction. My timing was perfect. I caught him shoulder height with my front claws. My front left paw's claws grabbed the arm of his t-shirt while my right paw's claws connected and buried in the flesh of his arm. The man was certainly caught off guard by my surprise gray brute attack! The newspaper flew out of his hands as he let out a blood-curdling scream. He grabbed his arm, which caused me to release my grip and slide back down to the ground.

The woman came running out of the kitchen and shouted, "What's wrong?"

The man was wincing in pain as he held his arm where my claws had landed. My nub of a tail was wagging enthusiastically the entire time as I knew that I had pleased him. He finally regained his composure and said, "PJ ambushed me for some reason!" The man looked down and glared at me. "Why did you attack me, girl?"

I responded by continuing to wag my tail.

He then shouted, "Geez, you're psychotic! You enjoyed that didn't you?"

His harsh tone of voice startled me a bit and I sat down and stared up at him.

The woman intervened. "Lower your tone. She doesn't understand why you're yelling at her." Her kind tone of voice comforted me. She then said, "Remember what you did last night when you fed her?" The man looked puzzled. The woman continued, "You kept riling her up by shouting 'are you ready for dinner?' Then when she didn't respond, you shouted it again. The third time, she knocked the food bowl out of your hand. She thought that you wanted her to attack you for her food." She looked down at me and patted my head, "Isn't that right, PJ?"

I licked her hand. *She has such a kind-hearted voice and demeanor. And she's smart.*

The man apparently could not believe what he was hearing. "I am the one who gets attacked, and suddenly I'm the culprit? There is no way in hell that she's smart enough to connect her response to my behavior last night with what she did this morning."

The woman smiled and responded, "This is the same girl that somehow managed to get from one side of the doggie fence to the other without jumping over it or knocking it down. I'm just saying!"

The man shook his head in apparent disbelief. He then said to me, "Girlfriend, no more ambushes, okay?" His voice was a lot softer than before.

I pretended to understand and wagged my tail ever so slightly. He seemed pleased with that response.

The man walked into the kitchen and I followed him very closely. In fact, I was so close that I could feel my whiskers occasionally rubbing on the calf of his left leg. He pulled the same stainless steel bowl out of a cabinet that he used for my dinner the night before. The man then removed a bag of meat smelling pellets from another cabinet and measured some out into the bowl. Before placing it in front of me, he looked down at me and said, "Be gentle this time."

While I listened to him speak, I never took my eyes off the bowl. The man walked over into another small room and placed it on the floor. Again, I followed very closely behind him. As soon as he placed the bowl on the floor, I immediately moved in to investigate. I sniffed the side of the bowl first and then the contents. *Yes, these are the same beef pellets from last night's meal. They are tasty enough, but this man has little imagination and creativity. Would it have been so hard to have put a little brie or sprinkled parmesan cheese on top to add a bit of flavor?*

The man left me to eat alone and went back into the kitchen. It took me less than a minute to consume the entire contents of the bowl. I spent another few seconds sniffing around the perimeter of the bowl to make sure that I had not missed any of the pellets. There was also a bowl of water placed a few feet from my food bowl. I walked over and sniffed it but then I remembered the pond out in the backyard. *While this water seems fresh enough to drink, I think that I prefer to wait until I get outside and drink some fresher water from the pond in the backyard.*

When I walked back into the den, the man had read my mind, because he was standing by the door that led onto the deck in the backyard. He looked down at me and asked, "Are you ready to take care of some business?" The man opened the door and followed me outside. We both walked over to the pond. I leaned over and started drinking out of the pond. While lapping up the water, I could hear the man laughing behind me. "Girl, why are you drinking out of my swimming pool? You walked right by a bowl of fresh water in the house that I'd just poured for you."

I may not know how long I was on the streets, but I still know how to take care of my needs. I may have come from aristocracy, but when I am hungry, I know how to find food and when I am thirsty, I can locate water. Well, that was the case at least until my accident...the woman with the cinnamon smell said I had been in an accident. I still don't remember anything about it. All I do remember is waking up on the table in the middle of the room with the strong antiseptic smells.

As soon as I was done drinking, I trotted out to the far reaches of the yard to find a perfect spot for my business. The man turned his head to look away to give me some privacy. When I was finished, I trotted passed the man up to the wood deck. Similar to before, I smelled the strong scent of rabbit. I surmised that there were several rabbits holed up under the deck.

The man walked passed me and towards the back door of the house. He opened the door and whistled in my general direction. I completely ignored him. *The smells around the base of the deck are way more interesting than this man's whistling skills.*

The man hollered at me in frustration, "PJ, I still can't believe you don't respond to a whistle. Did you learn any tricks at all in your prior life?"

What is this man saying? And why is he annoyed with me? He sure is temperamental. I decided to leave my investigation for another time and return to the house.

When the man and I reentered the house, a lovely smell was wafting out of the kitchen to the den. I rapidly walked through the den and through the passageway that led into the kitchen. The woman was stirring something in a pan on top of the cooktop. She smiled down at me as I approached and said, "You find something of interest here, PJ? I am not going to let you sample anything. You've just eaten. Why don't you go take a nap while we eat breakfast?" She gestured with the spatula in her right hand at the man. "If you're good, PJ, maybe old grumpy there won't feel compelled to lock you behind the doggie fence during our breakfast."

The man laughed and said, "She would probably just break it down or worse, do her Houdini act and somehow appear on our side. Which reminds me, after breakfast I need to check on the status of that dog crate I ordered online."

The woman responded, "That's good! She needs a proper place for her bed."

I was getting sleepy and decided to go back to the room where I slept last night. *I hope the man doesn't put that fence back up. Although, it's not much of an obstacle to overcome.* I walked over to my makeshift bed and spun around three times before finding the perfect position to nest. My stomach was full, I had fresh water from the pond, and had taken care of all my business. It was time for a brief morning nap. I could hear the man and woman talking in the kitchen but it was more comforting than bothersome. Before long, I was sound asleep.

I woke to the sound of dishes being placed on the

counter in the kitchen. The man shouted, "PJ, remember what I told you last night?"

What does the man want now? I stepped off my makeshift bed, shook and then stretched first my front paws and then my back legs. *There is still a great of deal of pain, but I must admit, it's significantly less than yesterday. I am definitely on the mend.* I walked briskly into the kitchen.

The man was alone at the sink rinsing dishes. When he heard the nails of my claws reverberating on the hardwood floors, he stopped what he was doing and turned around to face me. We made eye contact and he reached for something on the counter and picked up a morsel of what appeared to be bacon. I took a few steps closer to get a better look, but the scent was unmistakable. He extended the morsel towards my nose and said, "As I said before, I always save something from my meal for my dog." I snapped it cleanly out of his hand before he could change his mind.

He is definitely a Dr. Jekyll and Mr. Hyde kind of guy. One minute he is yelling at me, and the next he is giving me bacon. If not for the woman, I would have opted out of the agreement by now. Nonetheless, he does have his moments. I'll give him at least another day. After all, I have up to a week to decide whether this whole adoption thing is in my best interest or not. I still can't believe this guy used to practice law since he clearly seems not to understand contract law.

The man returned to cleaning dishes and I adjourned back to my makeshift bed. *I hope the man doesn't renege on another one of his promises to me.... I need a real bed. A blanket resting on top of a worn out pillow is not a proper bed for someone of my aristocratic background. I just wish I could remember that background.*

I went to take another morning nap. This time when I woke, both the man and the woman were staring down at me. Suspecting that they wanted my attention, I stood up and stepped off of my makeshift bed and performed my usual stretch...first the front paws and then my back legs. The man said, "PJ, we're going out for a while. I'm wondering if we can trust you. I'm thinking not. You will have a new dog crate and a special bed soon. But in the meantime, we have to do what we have to do. We're going to put you, your blanket, and a bowl of water in this small bathroom while we're gone. You'll be just fine here. I promise we won't be gone long."

The man then grabbed my blanket and placed it in the small bathroom just outside of the room where I had slept. Then, he picked up my water bowl and also placed it on the floor in the bathroom. Finally, he went back into the kitchen and brought back some kind of bacon smelling treat with him. He said, "Girlfriend, I'm sorry to have to put you in here while we're gone. I'm just worried that you'll have separation anxiety issues if we leave you free to roam until we return." He grabbed me by the collar and I reluctantly followed him into the bathroom. He closed the door behind us and said, "PJ, this is a contract. By your agreeing to stay in this bathroom while we run errands, I'm giving you a bacon treat." He extended his hand with the treat towards my nose. I gave it a slight sniff, but did not take it. I just stared him in the eyes with my dilated pupils. He shook it in front of my face as if that made the treat more appealing.

I am not about to take that treat because I don't want to be confined in this bathroom while you're gone. What if you don't come back? What happens then?

The man gently set the treat down next to the water bowl and opened the door of the bathroom just enough so he could shimmy out. He kept his right leg between the door and me so that I could not follow him. He reopened the door slightly and peered in at me and said, "I'm sorry, girl! I will leave the light on though."

I heard the door latch click and I listened to the man's footsteps as he walked away. *This man had to be a horrible lawyer. He talks about confining me against my will in a tiny bathroom as a contract. If it's a contract, aren't I supposed to get something that I want out of it? Sure he offered me a bacon treat. Did I accept the treat? No! He set it on the floor. The contract that the man should be concerned about is our adoption agreement. He read the provision out loud, which stated I am to have free run of the house. But here I am...confined in a small prison cell.*

A few minutes later, I heard footsteps and heard the man and woman talking. *Maybe the woman will remind him of his contractual obligations.* The footsteps did not stop outside the door. They continued to the back of the house.

Sure enough, I was left all alone in this small bathroom. *What should I do?* I bumped the door with my nose but it did not give an inch. Next, I leapt up and put my front paws on the door. I dug my claws deep into the wood façade of the door and allowed gravity to pull my body back down to the floor. My claws left huge gashes in the door. I glanced over and noticed a full roll of toilet paper hanging on the wall. In a flash, I swatted at it with my left paw and it started to unravel and pile up on the ground. While I enjoyed watching the toilet paper pile up, I was no closer to freeing myself from this small prison cell. *Maybe there's another way out of here.*

I sniffed the floor and discovered a set of cabinets underneath a water faucet. One of the cabinet doors was slightly ajar. I was able to get my head inside just enough to pry it open. I decided to step inside to get a better look. There was nothing there except a stack of cans. My left shoulder grazed the stack, which caused the top can to tumble out of the cabinet onto the tile floor. When it struck the floor, its lid popped off and white paint began to ooze out. *Well, this is messy.* I had no choice but to step in the white paint in order to get back to the door. *I should try the door again.* I pounced upon it with my paint covered paws. My claws were so slippery with paint that they slid down the wood façade and collided with the doorknob. Apparently, they caught the doorknob just right because it unlatched and the door cracked opened a few inches. I was able to maneuver my nose into the crack and force my way through the door. It was nice to be free of that small bathroom.

Because of the paint, I had trouble keeping my footing on the hardwood floors and kept slipping. *I need to get this stuff off of the pads of my feet. I know what to do.* I walked through the kitchen and into the den. Slipping and sliding, I finally reached the rug in the middle of the room. I started rubbing my paw pads against the grain of the carpet. First one and then another. *This is working! Now there is more paint on the carpet than on my feet. Success!* I ventured off the rug to the hardwood floors. *Yes, much better traction this time.*

I decided it was time to see if there was a way out of the house. *I will start at one end of the house and conduct a search of every room.* When I entered one room at the end of the house, I could tell that the man spent a lot of time in there. I could smell his scent everywhere. It had a large desk covered with papers and other items. His desk was pushed up next to a window with wooden blinds, which were only partially drawn. The bottom of the window was about the same height as my head. A trash can rested next to the desk. *If I can just move it a tad, I think I will be able to look out of the window through the blinds.*

I nudged the trash can with my nose and pushed it just a few inches to the side. Now there was enough room for me to squeeze through to the window. My sight was still partially obstructed by the blinds. *If I could just get them to open a little, I could see so much better.* Careful to use the left side of my mouth, I grabbed the third to the lowest horizontal blind and forcefully bit down with my left canine tooth and shook my head several times. Finally, I felt the blind dislodge from the rest of the blinds and snap off into my mouth. Once I was certain it was separated from the rest of the blinds, I released my grip on it. My handiwork had left a jagged but gaping hole in the blinds. *Yes, much better. I can see clearly out the window and can survey the entire front property now.*

I went room by room, trying to find some means to escape. There was no obvious opening that I could detect regardless of which room I searched. *All this work has made me thirsty. I should go back and get a drink of water before I continue any further.* I walked back to the small bathroom where the man had placed my water bowl before closing the door and confining me. The door was still cracked open just enough for me to slip back through. I walked over and started lapping up the water. After I finished drinking, I remembered the bacon treat, which the man used to try and bribe me. *No point in letting it go to waste.* I immediately chewed and swallowed it.

As I was turning around to leave, my hind legs slipped on the paint that now covered most of the entire floor and my right buttocks bumped into the door, causing it to close. I heard the door latch as it closed. *Oh no, I just trapped myself again in this small prison cell. This won't do!* I threw all my weight against the door, but to no avail. It did not give an inch. *Maybe if I can hit the door knob just right...it will open like it did before.* I pounced time after time on the façade of the door, leaving huge scars and splatters of white paint on both the door and the surrounding wall. When I did manage to hit the door knob, it would jiggle a tad, but not quite enough for the door to open. Finally, my left paw hit dead center on the button that protruded in the middle of the doorknob, causing it to push in and click. Thereafter, whenever I was able to strike the door knob, it was immoveable and locked securely into position.

I was tired and suddenly very thirsty again. I walked over to my water bowl and lapped up the remaining water. Then I sat down in the corner of the small bathroom. *I guess I'll just try to calm myself down and hope the man and woman haven't forgotten about me.* I laid down on the only part of the floor now that was not covered in paint and closed my eyes. Within a matter of minutes, I was sound asleep. I am not certain how long I slept before I heard the noise of the door that leads to the garage open. Once again, I heard the sound of footsteps and the voices of the man and woman. It was dark outside the bathroom. It was night and the man and woman had not yet turned on the lights. I stared at the door handle and listened as the man attempted to open it from the other side.

He tried it several times without success. "PJ, are you okay? How did you manage to lock yourself in there?

I heard the woman scream from what I assumed was the kitchen. "Oh my, what happened in here?"

The man responded, "What do you mean, 'what happened?'"

She said, moving through the house, "Look at all these white paw prints leading from the bathroom, through the kitchen, and onto the den rug!"

The man joined her. "Did PJ do this?"

The woman responded, "That has to be her paw prints in paint, but I have no idea how she did it."

I heard the sound of footsteps as the man and woman walked back to the small bathroom. The man said, "She's locked herself in! There's no way she could have done this!"

The woman responded, "She must have gotten into the paint under the sink and then figured away to get out. But how she managed to lock herself in is beyond my imagination."

I was feeling scared and frustrated and started to whimper.

The man attempted to twist the doorknob, but it would not move. "Would you get me a paperclip and I'll try to pick the lock. If this doesn't work, I'll have to call a locksmith and a Sunday night service call isn't going to be cheap!"

From my side of the door, I heard the man tap on the doorknob and then occasionally attempt to turn the handle. After what seemed like an eternity, the knob finally turned. The man opened the door as wide as it would go. "Holy Shhhh!" the man screamed.

The woman then gently whispered, "Are you okay, PJ?" *She always seems to know what to say in a crisis.*

She then said, "Look, see the cabinet is open. She must have knocked over the can of paint when she tried to escape the bathroom. Poor girl! I bet she was scared to death."

The man responded, "That poor girl tracked paint throughout the house and ruined a $1,000 rug! I'm not sure that we're a good match." He then glared at me, "Remember, PJ, either party may void the agreement in the first week, no questions asked!"

While I waited with the man, the woman grabbed a roll of paper towels from the kitchen. When she returned, she started cleaning the white paint off of me. Meanwhile, the man started scrubbing on the walls with some sort of cleaner with an ammonia smell.

That was all the excitement I could handle for one day. I was both hungry and tired. The woman prepared my dinner while I watched.

I started to pounce on her like I did the man earlier but changed my mind. *She may not enjoy being attacked like the man. I suspect it is just a peculiar trait of his. No, I will save my pre-meal surprise attacks for the man.*

After dinner, she and I went into the den and I curled up on the hardwood floor next to the woman. It was a little uncomfortable lying on the bare floor; the man had removed the paint saturated carpet and placed it in the garage. The man then returned from the garage carrying the most beautiful and comfortable looking bed that I had ever seen. He walked over to where I lay and set it beside me. "Not sure we will make it through our trial period, girl, but at least you will be comfortable for a while anyway. While you were painting the house, we were out buying you a brand new bed."

I wagged my nub of a tail rapidly and immediately walked onto the bed. It felt very soft. I performed my signature three circles and dropped instantly into the cushioned contours of this wonderful bed. *I cannot remember, but I am absolutely certain that I had such a bed prior to the accident. My aristocratic upbringing must have had such a bed. The man is certainly a complex individual. One minute, he's screaming at me and threatening to void our agreement and the next, he's bringing me a heavenly bed.*

I was sound asleep when I heard the man scream, "PJ!" from the back of the house.

The woman was still sitting next to me. "What's wrong, now?" she asked in her calm voice.

The sound of heavy footsteps reverberated off the hardwood floors of the hallway as the man walked back towards the den. "This is what's wrong!" In his right hand was the fragmented part of the blinds from the back room. The man waved it at me and said, "She destroyed the blinds in my study! Look, she even managed to put some white paint on them for good measure."

The woman replied, "It's okay. We can always get new

blinds if necessary. Poor girl. She must suffer from separation anxiety."

The man let out a deep sigh. "We're the ones suffering from separation anxiety. We leave PJ by herself one time and she morphs into a $1,000 demolition monster."

The woman calmly responded, "PJ didn't like being locked up all alone in that small bathroom. She will be just fine when her crate arrives. We will just have to be patient with her until then."

The man dropped the fragmented blind next to my bed and said, "PJ, I'm not sure we can afford you."

I extended my neck from the safe confines of my new bed and sniffed the fragmented blind. *Yes, I recognize this. It is from the room that smelled like the man. I have no idea why he seems upset. He now has an unobstructed view out his window to the front of the house.*

The man picked up the twisted piece. "I am going to throw this away and get the new doggie fence out of the garage. It's time to go to bed."

The woman asked me, "PJ, would you like to go outside one more time?"

I immediately stood up on my bed and followed her over to the back door. We both went outside. It was a nice crisp night. Before taking care of my business, I trotted over to the pond to get one last drink of fresh water for the night. When we returned to the house, my bed was missing from the den. *The man hasn't taken my bed away has he? I know he was upset for some reason but that would be cruel and disrespectful. It would definitely be a deal killer as far as our agreement is concerned.*

We were not two steps inside the door when the man rounded the corner that separated the kitchen from the den. He said, "Okay, PJ, your bed is all set up in your room back there. Come on, girl."

I dutifully followed him to the back room. My bed was placed next to a sofa and underneath a window. There was another blanket on top of it. He patted my head, "I thought you might like an extra blanket in case it gets cold tonight."

I walked over, stepped on my bed, turned around three times, and plopped down. It felt wonderful and the new blanket was a nice touch, although it smelled a little bit like clothes detergent. *I'll have to work on that sometime.*

The man erected the fence in the same location as the previous night. He then erected an identical new fence on top of the old one. The whole structure was about six feet high. Obviously pleased with his handiwork, he said, "This ought to keep you in for the night." The man then switched off the light and walked away.

Why is he so obsessed with this barrier thing? I will worry about that later. I'm too tired now. I closed my eyes and went to sleep.

7

Day Three of the Trial Period

I woke up only once during the night. *I keep having this recurring dream of bright lights coming at me very fast. I am not quite sure what the lights are or where they are coming from. Before whatever it is collides with me, I wake up. It's scary. Am I dreaming about my accident? Was I hit by a car or truck?*

When I woke again, sunlight was streaming in through the partially closed window blinds. I stood up on my new bed and stepped off. First, I stretched my front legs and then the back ones. *I'm thirsty...and hungry.* I looked at the two barricaded fences the man had erected, intent on keeping me confined. *I recall from my occurrence yesterday, that there is a soft spot in the older fence.* I followed the same routine as last time and hit the lower metal contraption just right. Similar to my earlier experience, a gap formed at the bottom, which allowed me just enough room to crawl underneath it. When my hind legs cleared the fence, I stood up and once again my nub of a tail glanced it ever so slightly, causing it to close back up. Once again, it looked untouched.

I walked over to sniff the bowl of water. While I was sure the pond water outside was fresher, this was closer, so I lapped some up and then walked through the kitchen to the glass door in the den. It was the start of a beautiful day. The backyard looked very inviting. *I bet those rabbits are feeding in the garden. If I could just get outside, I would give them a run for their money. Oh well. I wonder what's happening out in the front yard?* I walked down the hallway to the room that smelled like the man and over to the window. The gaping hole in the blinds that I created yesterday provided an excellent vantage point. I not only saw the front yard, but all the way down the street since the house was situated on a corner.

In the distance, I could just make out the silhouette of a man and a handsome brown Labrador. I watched intently as they drew nearer. *They're within a few yards of my window; time to sound the alarm.* I barked ferociously for several seconds. My barking definitely got their attention even outside of the window. The man stopped and stared in my direction, and the brown Labrador responded with his own barking. *He is definitely a big, handsome boy!*

My barking also did not go unnoticed inside the house.

I heard the latch of the door to the man and woman's bedroom open. The man shouted, "PJ, where are you?"

I had no intention of taking my eyes off of the man and the handsome brown Labrador.

The man walked down the hallway in the opposite direction from where I stood. Apparently he thought that I was still in bed, barricaded from the rest of the house. He walked back down the hallway towards his bedroom and the room that I was in at the end of the hall. He shouted, "I can't find PJ!"

The woman replied, "What do you mean you can't find PJ? We definitely heard her bark."

Meanwhile, the man and the handsome Labrador had moved out of my sight. *I guess I'll go check out what all the excitement is with the man and woman in the hallway.*

When I exited the room that smelled like the man, the woman said, "There's PJ!"

The man glanced in my direction. "How the hell did you get out of two doggy fences, and what were you barking at?"

I just stood and stared at the man.

He continued his rant, "We've never heard you bark before and didn't even know that you could bark. How come you decided the perfect time to share your talents with us is at the crack of dawn when we we're sleeping?"

When he finally stopped talking, I stretched my front paws out on the hallway floor and pushed my rear end up in the air. The woman said, "Ah look, she wants you to play with her."

I straightened back up and walked by the couple into their bedroom and over to the door that led outside to the backyard.

The man said, "I think she wants to go outside and take care of her business." He walked over and opened the door for me.

I trotted the length of the deck but paused when I reached the end. The scent of rabbit was seemingly everywhere. I poked my nose under the deck and inhaled. *Yes, they're definitely under this deck.* After a few more obligatory sniffs, I headed out to the middle of the backyard to relieve myself. It was nice to be outside in the cool crisp air. *I might as well go get a drink of water out of the pond before I head back to the house for breakfast.* As I trotted by a small garden, which abutted the concrete walk that surrounded the pond, I heard something rustle in the garden. *This requires further investigation.*

As is my custom, I carefully placed one paw in front of the other with my nose a few inches off the ground. I slowly made my way through the garden, smelling every nook and cranny. When I had almost covered the entire garden, I heard some twigs snap to my right. I quickly looked up to see the white tail of a rabbit hopping furiously in the direction of the deck. *If my right leg wasn't still tender from my accident, I could've caught that rascal! Maybe in a few weeks we will meet again when the playing field is level.* I walked over to the pond and lapped up a bit of water. Before I had finished, the man shouted out from the back den doorway, "PJ, quit drinking from my pool and come in and get your breakfast!" *Ah, the magic word...breakfast!* I trotted back to the stairs that led up to the deck. *I think I'll be able to hurdle those shrubs to take a more direct route...probably in a few weeks when I am completely healed...if I decide to stay here.*

When I reentered the house, I smelled something wonderful in the air. The woman was standing in front of the range stirring something in a skillet. The man came in behind me and said, "PJ, your food is waiting for you in the utility room. I would have waited for you to arrive before I put it in your bowl, but I didn't want to give you an opportunity to attack me."

I wasn't quite sure what this utility room was all about. However, I relied on my nose to locate my breakfast. Although there were a lot of competing smells in the area, I located this utility room with no trouble. There sat a bowl of pellets with a nice bacon treat as a garnish on top. How thoughtful! *That must have been the woman's idea.* I was so enamored with my breakfast that I didn't notice the man watching me eat. He startled me when he asked, "PJ, did you like how I made your breakfast special this morning?" *I did like my breakfast, but I do not believe the bacon was his idea. Though he is a man of many contradictions...so it could be.*

After breakfast, I trotted back to the door. I wanted to

go back to the garden area to see if I could find that rabbit. The man opened the door for me and left the door slightly cracked behind me so that I could come back in without his assistance. I walked quietly across the deck, smelling in between the slats of wood every step. *Judging from the strong scent, there must be an entire family or families of rabbits down below. I always enjoy this type of investigation when my stomach is full of food. I don't remember the specifics, but I recall hunting for food prior to my accident.* I stepped off the deck onto the pavement and headed back to the garden where I had discovered the rabbit earlier this morning. I sniffed around a bit, but it wasn't to be found. *If the rabbit is still here, I'll find it.* I walked over to the pond and lapped up some fresh water before heading back to the house. When I discovered that the man had left the door cracked open for me, I shoved it forcefully with my head. In fact, the force caused it to bounce off the wall with a loud thud.

The man shouted from the other room, "PJ, take it easy on the door!"

I walked into the kitchen and into the dining room where the man and woman were eating their breakfast. I curled up and laid down in the doorway that separated the kitchen from the dining room. I was strategically positioned so that no one could enter the kitchen without stepping over me. *I guess the man has finally learned that attempting to confine me behind barriers is not only a breach of our agreement, but futile since I know how to break out.*

When the man and woman finished their meal, they

both stood up and stepped over me to get back to the kitchen. Similar to last evening, the man set his plate on the counter. He removed a morsel of bacon off his plate and waved it in my direction. "Here you, go girlfriend. As promised."

The man is an odd one, but I do like his tradition of saving something from his plate for the dog of the family. I crossed the kitchen to where he stood and gently removed the bacon from his hand.

He smiled down at me. "That's the way to take a treat, PJ. Good girl!"

8

The Great Escape

Later that morning, I was napping on my new bed when the woman entered the room. She walked directly over to my bed and kneeled down beside me. She extended her hand and patted my head. "I've got to go to work now. You mind the big guy while I am gone. He's not as grumpy as he appears."

She is always so calming. I leaned over and gave her hand a slight lick. *She smells nice.* After I heard the woman leave I thought, *I wonder what the man is up to? I'd better go find out.*

I walked the length of the house to the hallway that connected the bedrooms. The man was in his bathroom. I heard water running from his shower. He appeared to be enjoying himself because he was singing. *I wonder if he heard a fire truck? Sometimes when I hear a siren, I let out a howl that sounds like the man.* I snuck a peek over to the large platform bed that dominated the room. The unmade bed looked even more comfortable than my new bed. I could not resist taking a closer look. I hopped on the platform. The right side of the bed smelled like the man. *This must be where he sleeps. I am going curl up on his side of the bed and wait for him to finish in the bathroom.*

The water suddenly stopped running. Within a few minutes, the door of the bathroom opened and there stood the man in his boxer shorts. His eyes got huge when he saw me lying on his bed. He shouted, "PJ, get off my bed!"

I don't like the tone of his voice. I don't think he approves of me being on his bed. I'd better leave. Before he could reach me, I sprinted across the bed to the other side and jumped off and exited the bedroom. The man did not follow, but I heard the sound of the bedroom door slamming behind me.

I decided to wait at the end of the hallway to see what the man did next. I wanted to keep an eye on his whereabouts but not too close if he was still angry. I curled up on the hardwood floor, which was not too comfortable but it did provide a good vantage point. After several minutes, the man opened the bedroom door. He was fully dressed and walked toward me. I could tell from the expression on his face, that he was still angry with me for some reason.

"PJ, what am I going to do with you? You have got to

learn not to get on the furniture, which also includes my bed. Do you understand?"

I sat motionless and stared at him. The man leaned towards me. I thought he might hit me, but I held my ground and resisted the urge to growl at him. That was smart thinking on my part, because instead, he patted me on the head, which baffled me. "PJ, I have to run some errands. So, what am I going to do with you? It's a beautiful day and you should be enjoying being outside. I can't put you in the backyard though because the guy cleans the pool today. I imagine that you would be okay with that but I am not sure I can trust you yet. Another option is that I can put you in the small bathroom, but we both know how that can turn out. The only other option is to put you in the side yard." He motioned for me to follow him. The man opened a glass door that led from the kitchen onto a small wood deck. He stepped out first and walked across the deck to a narrow yard that was surrounded by a large fence on two sides. The house was on one side and a gate was on the fourth side.

"What do you think, PJ? Is staying out here better than being locked in the small bathroom?"

I sniffed around a bit and surveyed the area. I could smell rabbits and a dog next door.

The man said, "You seem to be okay with this option." He walked back onto the deck and opened the door to the kitchen. "I think you will be just fine out there. I'll only be gone for a couple of hours."

I also would be just fine on my bed in the house. However, that would require you to trust me. If you want me to trust you, then you have to trust me.

I watched as the man filled my water bowl at the kitchen sink. Once it was full, he placed it on the side deck. He then rummaged through a drawer with his right hand and found a bag. When he opened it, I could immediately smell the unmistakable beef smell of a treat. The man opened the door to the side yard and I followed behind him. He reached down and handed me the treat. I sniffed it and then gently took it from his hand. "Good girl! You will be just fine out here until I get back. It's a beautiful day to take a nap in the shade over there." The man pointed to a grassy shaded area next to the house. He then went back into the house.

At first, I just sat on the deck and pondered my next move. *So, is he going to leave me out here all by myself?* I decided to get the lay of the land. I started at one end of the narrow yard and sniffed the perimeter of the large fence. I made my way to the back of the side yard, where there was a wooden gate with slates that separated the yard from the driveway. *Even if I get out of this gate there is still the large gate on wheels that borders the property on the alley that separates me from freedom. I remember the man hit some kind of button in his car to open that monstrous thing when he first brought me home.* I watched through the slats in the gate as the man backed his car out of the garage and waited for the large gate to open. When his car cleared the track of the gate into the alley, the large gate closed behind him.

Time for me to go to work. Even with just a cursory investigation of the confined area, I knew instantly that the two gates provided the only potential means to escape. I sniffed the gate and gave it a nudge with my nose. It did not give an inch. I examined the gate's latch, which was, I'm pretty sure, meant to fit snuggly into the cylinder of the support post next to it. But what I noticed was that the latch was positioned slightly off and rested right next to the cylinder. I couldn't determine why the latch and cylinder did not line up, but the man obviously knew about it because he had addressed this problem with two bright orange bungee cords wrapped tightly several times around the post and through the gate.

Upon closer inspection, I saw that the bungee cords were very taut and resisted any pressure to move the gate. *I wonder if I can chew through these cords?* It took a great deal of strategy and maneuvering to get the first cord into position. I had to balance both front paws on the gate latch and turn my head as far left as possible. That enabled me to clench the first cord with the left side of my mouth. *I'm pretty sure that I have chewed through many a leash in my time. Maybe that's even how I started my adventure on the streets. Pit bulls have nothing on me. Nothing will distract me until I am successful.* I continued to gnaw and bite the first orange bungee cord. When it started to slightly frazzle, I became even more determined and animated. *Just a few more gnaws and bites should do the trick.* After around thirty minutes, the bungee cord snapped in two and fell harmlessly to the ground. *Only one to go!*

I started the same procedure on the second bungee cord. With the first one out of the way, I had better access to the second cord. In less than twenty minutes, I gnawed, chewed, and bit my way through the second cord. Part of it fell to the ground on top of the other severed cord and part of it remained wrapped around the post. The gate was completely unattached from the post. With only a light nudge with my nose, the gate swung open. *I would love to hang around and see the expression on the man's face when he returns and sees the chewed up bungee cords and the wide open gate. However, I don't know for certain if he or the woman are going to return. I think she probably will because she really seems to care about me. The man is just way too unpredictable.*

I walked through the open gate onto the driveway and over to the massive gate on wheels. There was about a four-inch gap between the bottom of the gate and the track to allow for the wheels of the gate to roll. *There is no way that I can squish under the gate. It is way too narrow.* I decided to walk the length of the gate to see how it connected to the fence when it closed.

There was about an eight-inch gap between the gate and fence. *I might just be able to squeeze through if the gate will give just a tad. The weight that I lost during my accident might just have a silver lining. I'm going to go for it.* I stuck my head and shoulders through the gap between the gate and fence and pushed with all the force I could muster with my back legs. Sure enough, the gate gave ever so slightly and I ended up in the alley. *I am free at last!*

My freedom was not without cost. In the process of clearing the fence and gate, my front knee caught temporarily on the gate. I knew instantly that I had slightly aggravated my still healing leg. Although it was a bit painful, I could still get around, but it caused me to limp. *So, what do I do now?* I spent some time sniffing around the trash cans. There was a variety of food smells. *I wonder if the brie cheese is in there.* I decided to take a closer look. I reared up and placed my front paws on the lid of the trashcan. The lid was on tight. *This is of no use. I cannot possibly get that lid off. Even if I knock it over, I doubt that the lid will come off.*

I decided to give up and explore the rest of the alley. About ten yards down and across the alley was a neighbor's trashcan. I made my way over to it, sniffing the ground all the way to it. There were interesting smells also emanating from the top of this can. I reared up on it and quickly discovered that it had no lid. My front paws caught the front edge of the trashcan, which caused it to topple forward under my weight. It crashed down, spilling all its contents into the middle of the alley. I was extremely disappointed to discover very little food that was salvageable. The contents consisted primarily of glass wine bottles, which shattered on contact with the pavement of the alley.

I quickly grew bored and decided to move on with my investigation. Still limping, I walked the length of the alley, which intersected the street that ran along the side of the man and woman's house. I decided to cross the street to check out the alley on the next block. A car drove passed me as I began to step into the street. It paused so I decided to pick up my pace a bit and trotted to the next alley. It, too, was lined with trash cans. I walked the entire length of the alley, sniffing and sampling a few bits of food that had spilled out. When I turned the corner of the alley, my nose picked up a very pungent smell. About twenty yards down the alley, several large black birds were standing over the carcass of what appeared to be a squirrel. When the birds noticed me moving towards them, they squawked and flew to a nearby tree and stared down at the carcass.

The closer I drew, the stronger the smell of death became. My breed is known for its stalking skills. I can spend literally hours stalking my prey. *There will only be one of two outcomes, either my prey will escape or I will catch it. I will never quit mid-stalk for any reason. However, I have learned that in order to successfully stalk, you must have the element of surprise. Your prey cannot sense that you are there until it is too late. Most prey have a keen sense of smell, which allows them to always be on alert even if they are busy at another task such as searching for food. When you smell like your prey, they cannot smell you. Since I may be on the streets for a while, I better be prepared to stalk again for my food.* I limped over to where the carcass lay. Left shoulder first, I rolled over on the carcass and rubbed back and forth on my back. I was successful because my fur began to absorb the pungent smell of the dead squirrel.

9

Shocking Discovery

Of course I was not there, but I later heard that this is what happened when the man came home:

The man pulled his Mini Cooper into the alley, came to a screeching stop, and exited the car. The alley was littered with broken wine bottles. He got out of his car and stared at the debris in the alley. "What happened here?" he asked. He righted his neighbor's trash can and began carefully picking up the broken glass. He said to no one in particular, "I guess a car or truck knocked it over. I can't believe that they didn't bother to pick it up though." He spent about ten minutes cleaning up the alley and then got back in his car and drove towards the large gate on wheels that separates the alley from his driveway. As was his custom, he hit the remote control first for the gate and

---

again for the garage. When there was room for his car to clear the gate, the man hit the remote again and the gate closed behind him.

He cast a glance over to the side yard where he had secured me a few hours earlier. "What the hell? How did the gate get opened?" The man pulled his car into the garage and parked it. In a matter of seconds, he was standing at the open gate, gaping speechlessly. He reached down and clasped the shredded piece of the bungee cord that was still hanging on the open gate. Without any further hesitation, he jogged from the gate to the other end of the side yard and hollered "PJ! Where are you?"

When there was no response, the man walked back out of the open gate, onto the driveway, and then over to the large gate on wheels. He stopped and scratched his bald head. "How did she get out of here?" He knelt down and peered under the small gap between the bottom of the gate and its tracks. "There's no way she could get under this gate." He stood up and sighed, "I am going to be in so much trouble!"

He went back to his car, picked up the remote control for the large gate, pressed the button, and watched as the gate slowly ambled along the track. When it was wide enough for him to step through, the man walked into the alley. He then closed the gate behind him and started walking down the alley the way he had just driven in. With every step he took, his eyes darted right and then left, looking for his wayward dog. When the man reached the point where the alley intersected the street that ran by the side of his house, he came across a woman walking a black Labrador. "Excuse me," he said, "have you possibly seen a gray female Weimaraner?"

The woman with the black Labrador shook her head side to side. "No, sorry. Does she have a collar and a tag?"

The man responded, "She only has a collar and a rescue tag. She's a rescue dog and we just got her. I ordered a personalized tag, but it hasn't arrived yet."

The woman with the black Labrador did not respond but gave the man an incredulous look. The man was sure she was thinking: *How could you be so stupid as to leave your newly adopted dog unattended without a personalized tag?* He sighed and then continued on, walking the neighborhood block by block, at times calling out, "PJ, where are you?"

Dejected, the man walked back to his home. He went down the alley and through the large open gate that separated the alley from his driveway. Using the remote control, he opened and closed the large gate several times as if watching it open and close would provide some clue. He thought, *How could she have possibly gotten out of this gate. And why?* The man got into his car and retraced his steps, but there was still no sign of me. He drove around and scoured several blocks of the neighborhood. After about thirty minutes he deemed his search futile and returned home.

He sat in his car for a few minutes. "I am going to have to call Sharon and tell her what has happened." The man entered the house through the garage. As he walked through the room where PJ slept, he glanced over at the empty bed. His heart sank. The man then walked through the kitchen and sat down in one of the chairs in the den. He pulled his cellphone out from his coat pocket. He stared down at the bare, hardwood floor where the expensive rug that PJ destroyed with white paint had previously laid and dialed his wife's cellphone. It went straight to voicemail and he figured she was in some type of meeting. Instead of leaving a voicemail, he decided to send her a text message: "So sorry. PJ's missing! I left her in the side yard while I went to have my MRI. When I returned, she was gone. I can't find her anywhere."

The man set down his cellphone. He sat, crestfallen, and slumped into his chair.

10

On the Streets

I rubbed my back into the squirrel's carcass a few more times and then stood up. When I shook, I could smell the squirrel's scent on my fur. *Yes, I am ready to stalk for food.* I continued the direction that I was initially going down the alley. After walking a few more yards, the alley intersected another street. *I think I will check out some of the yards down this street.* At a distance, I could just make out what appeared to be a child spinning around in her front yard. *She is not that interesting and there are no appealing scents in the immediate area either, but I want a closer look at her.* Still limping, I slowly made my way towards the child. As I drew nearer, I could tell the little girl was dressed in sequins. She was completely absorbed in her own world, spinning round in circles and singing.

When I was about ten feet from her, the little girl came to a screeching halt. I watched as she stood still, facing in the opposite direction, and all the while sniffing the air. *She can't be smelling me because I smell like my prey. I wonder what's she is smelling. I hope its food!* The little girl then abruptly turned around and faced me. I remained motionless. She had a terrified expression on her face. Without prior warning, she screamed at the top of her lungs, "Mommy!"

At first, I did not notice a woman kneeling next to the flowerbeds near the front door of her house. She was facing in the opposite direction and busy digging in her garden. After the little girl screamed, she jerked her head around. The little girl was pointing with her right hand directly at me. The woman slowly rose to her feet. "What's the matter, dear? Is the dog scaring you?"

The little girl responded, "He stinks!"

He stinks? First, I am most definitely not a "he," and secondly, I do not stink!

The woman crossed the yard and joined the little girl a few feet from me. She replied, "You're right. He's probably harmless, but we need to be careful. Obviously, he appears to have been mistreated. Let's go in the house and I'll call animal control."

As they walked towards the house, the little girl inquired, "What's animal control?"

The woman responded, "They come and pick up stray dogs and keep them locked up."

I didn't like the sound of this animal control. No one was going to lock me up. I waited for the woman and the little girl to enter the house before I took off as quickly as my hurt leg would allow.

After limping almost to the end of the street, I noticed a fence to my right attached to a house on one side. The fence had become a little worse for wear. Several slats were missing at the bottom. *I wonder if there is anything interesting behind that fence? It would sure be nice to find a pond like the man and woman have in their backyard. I could use some fresh water.* I slowly meandered over to the fence, sniffing along the ground. *Some kind of dog has been here earlier.*

When I approached the opening in the slats, I came face to face with a German Sheppard. Upon seeing me, he began to growl in a deep base tone. Suddenly, he started barking and baring his teeth at me. In an act of friendliness, I bowed my head to the ground and stuck my rear end into the air. The German Sheppard was unconvinced. He continued barking angrily at me. *This is not the type of reception that I am accustomed to receiving. I'd better retreat back to the street.* My actions seemed to trigger some kind of obsession with the German Sheppard. *Maybe if I can get out of his eyesight, he will quit barking and go back to doing whatever he was doing before I came along.* I limped across the street. Although I knew that he could no longer see me, he continued to bark, which was only interrupted by the sound of him ramming his head into the opening in the slats. *I think he is trying to break out and come and get me. What should I do? I'm going to go hide behind those bushes.*

As I approached the bushes, I could smell cats. *No time to investigate now. I need to get out of sight and fast.* I pushed through a crease in the bushes and found a nice space to peer out so that I could see but not be seen. After a few minutes, the barking suddenly got louder.

The German Sheppard had successfully broken through the fence and was making his way to the street from the side of the house. I froze and tried to remain calm. The German Sheppard did not seem to notice where I had gone, because he took off in a dead run down the street that I had come up earlier.

He obviously isn't adept at stalking his prey; otherwise, he would've stopped to pick up a scent before randomly committing to one direction. He's got all the self-discipline of that gray brute.

Just when I thought it was safe to exit the bushes, I saw the German Sheppard run in the opposite direction down the street. *That's strange behavior.* Following close behind was a white truck. *I better stay put to see how this plays out.* No more than five minutes later, the German Sheppard once again sprinted in the opposite direction, but this time he turned and headed towards where I was safely concealed out of sight. Similar to me, he must have thought these bushes would provide a nice hiding place. A man in a blue uniform was now on foot in pursuit; the white truck followed him. The German Sheppard hesitated just slightly in front of the bushes. That moment of hesitation cost him dearly. The man in the blue uniform caught up and quickly slipped a loop attached to a pole over the German Sheppard's head. The man with the blue uniform shouted, "Got him! Open the back door!" The driver of the truck opened the back door to the truck and the man with the blue uniform led the German Sheppard into the back of his truck. The driver shut the door and both he and the man in the blue uniform got into the truck and drove away.

Wow, that was close. Not only did the German Sheppard almost get me, but also those guys in the truck. I better start searching for some water and food.

I walked down the street in the direction that I initially came. *I wonder if the man and woman ever came back to their home? It would have been nice if the man had trusted me so that I wouldn't have had to escape. A drink of water from the pond in the backyard would sure be nice right now. Maybe, I will try and find my way back to their house.* I tried to retrace my steps. *I think this is the alley with the squirrel carcass.* I entered the alley and began to walk as briskly as I could manage with my reinjured front leg. When I rounded the corner of the alley, I anticipated that I would be able to see the squirrel carcass. Unfortunately, there was no squirrel in sight.

I continued to make my way down the alley. A wooden gate to my left swung open and banged into the fence. An elderly man then pushed his trashcan on wheels through the opening of the gate and positioned it next to the fence. When the elderly man turned to go back into the gate opening, he looked down and we made eye contact. He smiled at me. "What have we got here?" He walked over to me and stopped a few feet away. "Oh my, dog, what did you get into? You need a hosing down something awful." He walked back to his gate, then stopped and motioned towards me. "Come on, dog, I'll give you some food and water. It won't be so bad."

Food! The magic word! I followed him through the gate into his backyard and up to his back porch. He opened the door to the back of his house slightly and shouted inside, "Hun, we got some company."

An elderly woman appeared at the backdoor. She said, "I was wondering who would come visiting us through the alley and now I understand. She must be lost. Oh, and look how she's limping."

She started to approach me when the elderly man cautioned, "Don't get too close, she's gotten into something unpleasant. Most likely, she found something dead to roll in. I love dogs dearly, but I never understood why they get so much pleasure out of smelling so bad."

The elderly woman responded, "She seems to have a collar and a tag."

The elderly man said, "I'll check it after I bathe her. Let's get her some water and food first so she'll trust me."

The woman reentered the house and returned a short time later with something on a plate that smelled wonderful. She set the plate down in front of me. "It's only our table scraps from lunch, but I think you will find them to your liking."

She was right. I quickly consumed all the morsels of food on the plate and licked it completely clean. While I was eating, the elderly man had filled a bowl of water and set it next to the plate.

These seem to be nice folks! They knew that I was hungry and thirsty.

After dinner and a nice drink of water, the elderly woman emerged from the house with a bucket of warm water and some shampoo. She set it on the back sidewalk. The elderly man walked over to the bucket and kneeled down. "Come on, girl. It is time you smelled like a proper young lady."

Although, I am certain that I come from aristocracy, I abhor baths. How can I stalk prey if I smell of gardenia, vanilla, or whatever scent emanates from this shampoo? On the other hand, these folks didn't have to feed me or give me water. I guess I can find another dead carcass to roll in. I reluctantly walked over to where the elderly man was kneeling.

"You're going to like this better than you think," he said.

He unbuckled my collar and then he reached into the bucket and pulled out a sponge full of warm water and started bathing me from head to tail. *I have to admit that the warm water and rubbing on my fur feels comforting.* Just when I was getting used to the bathing, the elderly man dropped the sponge in the bucket and turned the garden hose on me.

Whoa! Wait just a minute there! The water from the hose was ice cold. The elderly man ignored my protests and hosed me down for what seemed like an eternity. He held onto the scruff of my neck so that I could not run away. The elderly woman handed the elderly man a towel and he dried me thoroughly. As soon as he stopped, I took a few steps and vigorously shook. When I looked back at the elderly man, he was reading the tag on my collar. "It doesn't say who she belongs to only that she is sterile."

The elderly woman inquired, "Do we still have Nellie's old leash?"

The elderly man sighed. "Poor old Nellie. Now she was a good dog. Yes, I think it is hanging in my tool shed. Let me go check." The elderly man walked to an old shed in the back of the yard. The fifty-year-old hinges creaked and moaned as he opened the wood slatted door. The elderly woman and I watched as he walked back out of the shed. He was holding a dilapidated leash. He walked up and hooked it to my collar. "It's not pretty, but it will do in a pinch. Come on, girl, let's see if we can find your people. I'll take it slow with your sore front leg." The man led me through the house, which smelled like a combination of mildew and mothballs, and out the front door. "Let's sit here on the front porch a bit and enjoy the day."

11

The Dreaded Phone Call

I was enjoying my time with the older couple, and did not know if the man and woman even missed me. I did find out later what transpired when she learned I was not at home.

The man's silence was abruptly interrupted when his cell phone started buzzing. He glanced down and saw "Sharon" scroll across its screen. He picked it up and said, "Hey, so sorry!" He listened for a moment "You want to know how she got out of the house?" The man went into a lengthy explanation about how it was a pretty day and that he thought he could leave me in the side yard and how I managed to chew through two bungee cords and shimmy through the large gate on wheels. He continued to explain how he had walked and driven around the neighborhood, but to no avail.

The woman listened patiently to the man's explanation. "Well, I have one more meeting and then I'll come home to help look for her."

He felt as though he had failed her and responded, "Let me go out one more time and see if I can find her before you come home."

The woman replied, "Okay, but call and let me know."

He sighed, "Will do."

As soon as the man hung up the phone, he stood up and walked over to the closet where the leash was kept. He thought, "I am going to be optimistic and take the leash with me this time." Leash in hand, he started walking around the block. As soon as he rounded a curve in the street, the man saw at a distance, a man sitting on his front porch and a gray dog sitting on the concrete next to him. The man murmured, "Can that be PJ?" He quickened his pace, and moved toward the man and gray dog. When he was a few yards away, he called out, "PJ!" The elderly man and I cast a glance in the man's direction and when I saw him, I thought, *I am going to give him the cold shoulder for leaving me alone and locking me in the side yard.* I looked nonchalantly in the other direction.

The elderly man studied the man and then stared down at me to see how I reacted. "This your dog?"

The man walked up to the elderly man and me and paused before reaching us. "Yes, sir. She broke out of the fence this morning."

The elderly man rubbed his nose before responding.

"She doesn't have a tag, and I don't mean to be insensitive but she doesn't seem to know you either."

The man grimaced. "She's a rescue dog. My wife and I have only had her a couple of days. We haven't gotten fully acquainted yet."

The elderly man reached down and patted my head and asked me, "Do you know this man?"

I looked up and made eye contact with the man, but did not move another muscle.

The elderly man said, "I have to agree...you're not fully acquainted yet."

Frustrated, the man responded, "Sir, if you will pull up her right lip, you will notice that she is missing her right canine tooth and the one next to it."

The elderly man followed the man's instruction. "Poor girl. She must have gotten hit by a car or something. She was also limping pretty badly when she arrived at my back gate."

The man nodded. "That's what we thought as well."

The elderly man smiled. "I bet you don't know one thing about her."

"What's that?" the man asked, puzzled.

The elderly man responded, "She must have gotten into something after she left your place because she smelled like death when she greeted me in the alley a while ago. After feeding her, my wife and I gave her a bath."

"Uh oh, that is her second meal in less than three hours.

But, thank you for taking care of her." The man approached me and extended his hand to my nose.

I sniffed his coffee-smelling hand. *At the very least, you should have brought along a treat. Oh well, I suppose I should give him a little slack since we're in our trial period.* I slightly wagged my nub of a tail. That slight gesture seemed to satisfy both men.

The man said, "PJ, would you like to go home?" He slipped the leash onto my collar. I stood up. The man said, "Thanks again for taking care of her."

The elderly man nodded, "You two had better get better acquainted."

As we walked away, the man responded, "We will."

12

The Crate Arrives

The man and I walked slowly back down the street to his house. I was looking forward to a drink of water out of the pond in the backyard. He said, "PJ, why did you break out of the side yard? You know, you got me in a lot of trouble! I need to let Sharon know that you're okay."

He pulled his cellphone out of his pocket and momentarily stopped walking so that he could run his fingers across its screen. "Hey, sorry to bother you." There was a pause. "Yes, believe it or not, I found her." Again, there was a pause. The man laughed out loud. "She found an elderly couple down the street. Apparently, she had quite an adventure today, complete with rolling on some kind of dead carcass." He continued to talk with intermittent pauses. "Okay, we'll see you later." He finished his call and put the cellphone back into his pocket.

It was a beautiful day to be on a walk. Although, my leg hurt a bit, it was worth being out on an adventure. As we approached the man's house, I spotted a large parcel on the front porch. The man said, "PJ, I think your new crate has arrived." We both walked briskly across the front yard to the porch. "Yes, ma'am. It's your new crate." With me still on a leash, he unlocked the door and managed to push a huge box just inside the front door. He quickly unsnapped the leash from my collar.

I am thirsty from all this activity. I wish he would let me out so I could get some fresh water from the pond in the backyard. I walked over to the door in the den that led out into the backyard. The man was busy looking for something in the kitchen drawers. Finally, he walked back into the den, and I reached up and dragged my claws down the door. That got his attention.

"Girlfriend, do you want to go outside?" He opened the door and I trotted with my slight limp along the deck, once again noticing the scent of rabbits. "Please do not break out again. This is your huge backyard. I promise not to put you in the side yard again."

When I reached the edge of the deck, I hesitated and gently stepped onto the garden area. *Yes, the rabbits are definitely under this deck.* I sniffed around a bit. *I'm thirsty. The rabbits can wait.* I made my way to the big pond and started to lap up water. Once my thirst was quenched, I walked over to a shady, grassy area and rolled back and forth on my back. It needed a good rub to get rid of that freshly bathed feeling. I then stretched out on the grass a moment to reflect on the events of the day, thus far. *The man continues to baffle me. When he found me with the elderly man on the porch, he did seem sorry for his earlier actions. I can't figure him out. One minute he is locking me in solitary confinement and the next he is scouring the neighborhood looking for me. I wonder what he is doing now.* I rose to my feet and trotted back to the den door. For once, I decided to ignore the rabbits. When I got to the back door, I waited patiently for the man to let me in. I could not see him through the glass. *Surely, he hasn't abandoned me again!* I scratched the wooden part of the door with my right paw. Still, the man was nowhere in sight. Once again, I scratched the wooden part of the door, which did the trick.

The man appeared and opened the door. "Sorry, PJ, I was checking out your new crate."

I followed him into the living room. There was a large brand new crate sitting next to an empty box. "Let's move it to the back room and then you can check it out." I watched as he struggled to lift the crate and begin to walk. "Wow, this is heavy!" *This should be interesting.* I followed him as he slowly panted his way to the back room. The man had to stop several times and set the crate down. Finally, he reached the back room and slid the crate underneath a window. He grimaced as he straightened. "This should be a good place. What do you think, PJ?"

I walked over and sniffed the crate. There was no padding inside, so I elected not to investigate further. Instead, I walked over to my wonderful bed and spun three times before settling in.

I kept an eye on the man as he arranged some padding and an old dilapidated blanket inside the crate. When he had finished, he looked over at me. "Girlfriend, this crate looks pretty good to me. Most of the time, you can choose between your crate and your bed. It's only when it's necessary that I'll put you in the crate and lock the door." The man then went to the closet and returned with another thin blanket. He carefully covered the entire crate with the thin blanket except for the door.

What are you doing? First, you carefully position the crate below the window so that I'll get to wake up every morning to daylight and then you go and cover it up. That's not going to work. I prefer sleeping on my beautiful bed.

The man was obviously pleased with his handiwork. "See, PJ? I've given you some privacy. You can curl up in your crate and no one will be able to see you. Isn't this great, girlfriend?"

Better to just ignore him. Such foolishness! I let out a groan and shifted slightly in my bed to punctuate my disinterest. *I'm too tired to keep up with the whereabouts of the man.*

After napping for a couple of hours, I woke up. *I better go check and make sure the man didn't abandon me again. I* walked through the kitchen, the den, and the hallway that led to the bedrooms and the room that smelled like the man at the end of the hall. As soon as I entered the hall, I heard music coming from the room that smelled like the man. *He must be in his room.* I walked the length of the hallway. The man must have heard my nails clicking each time that I took a step on the hardwood floor.

When I entered the room, he said without looking up, "Hey, PJ, did you get a good nap?" The man was staring at a blue screen and clanking on the keys of a computer with his fingers. It was late in the afternoon and I could feel the beginning signs of hunger pangs in my stomach. *I wonder when I am going to get to eat again. I haven't eaten since the nice elderly couple fed me some table scraps a few hours ago. What to do?* I walked up and sat on the floor next to the man. He just continued to bang his fingers on the keyboard and stare at the blue screen.

He is a little slow to pick up on things. I should nudge him to let him know that I at least need a snack if not my dinner. I bumped his left arm with my nozzle.

"Not now, PJ. I'm busy."

Not to be ignored, I bumped him a second time with my muzzle.

"Do you want to go outside?"

Well, first choice is dinner. But, I'll take outside over standing next to you just staring at the blue screen. I walked over to the door that led out onto the side yard and tapped the doorknob slightly with my nose.

"Okay, okay, I'll let you outside." The man stood up, walked over, and opened the door so that I could go outside.

I walked a few minutes and decided to stretch out in the sun. *The heat on my freshly bathed coat felt heavenly.* I lay stretched out on my belly for several minutes before rolling onto my back to give it a good scratching. I stood up and as is my custom, shook vigorously. It was then that I heard that dreadful sound. That sound jarred some kind of horrific memory that had been locked in my brain. *What is causing that sound?* I trotted over to the wooden gate and peered through the crack between the gate and the supporting post. From my vantage point, I just caught a glimpse of a truck as it drove slowly by the house and parked just across the street. *I remembered! That is the same kind of truck I encountered the night of my accident. I cannot recall precisely what happened, but the consequences are obviously unpleasant. All that I can remember is that noise and bright lights. The next thing I remember is lying on that metal table in the middle of the room with the strong antiseptic smell.*

I decided to bark to express my displeasure. I let out a bloodcurdling ferocious series of barks.

The man heard my barking and quickly swung the door open. "Wow, PJ, what's the matter?" I ignored the man and continued barking through the crack in the gate. The man walked over by the gate where I stood. He joined me in staring at the truck across the street. As I growled, the man seemed to understand that I was upset. He reached down and patted my head. "Good girl! Thanks for keeping us safe from that UPS truck. There's no telling what sinister items he is delivering to our neighbors."

I looked up at the man. *Pretty impressive barking, huh? I'm most certainly a princess, but I do know how to fend for myself if necessary.*

"Let's go inside, girlfriend and give the delivery guy and the rest of the neighborhood some peace and quiet." The man opened the door and waited for me to enter first.

I know that I've already had two breakfasts this morning, but I am really starting to get hungry. I may be a little underweight, but there's nothing wrong with my appetite. Much to my disappointment, the man went back over to his desk and sat down. *He must be easily amused. I have never seen anyone so content tapping their fingers and staring at a blue screen.* I walked over and bumped the man's right arm with my muzzle.

"PJ, what is it this time?" he said without looking up from the screen. Then he paused and looked down at me. "I am pretty sure that the evil UPS truck is gone by now. Do you need to go back outside?" I stared at him and licked my chops. "Oh, you're hungry. Is that it?" He looked at his wristwatch and said, "Give me a few more minutes and then I will feed you your dinner."

He may be slow. However, I heard the word dinner in there somewhere. I'll go wait for him in the den. If he shows up in a timely manner, I'll reward him with something I know he enjoys. I walked out of the man's room down the hallway towards the den. The man shouted, "PJ, I'll just be a minute or two."

I positioned myself in the den where the rug used to be before the man removed it because of a little paint that happened to be on my paws—by accident. The man could not walk into the kitchen without walking within a few feet from where I was located. I hunkered down with my front paws extended and my hind legs tucked underneath ready to pounce. *I'm ready! Now, all I have to do is just wait for my prey to walk by.* After a few minutes elapsed, the man rose from his chair and continued on the path to the kitchen. He was so preoccupied that he did not even acknowledge my presence.

This is almost too easy. On the other hand, if this is what he enjoys, then so be it. I waited until the man was no more than three feet away from me and then sprung to my feet, and without hesitation, leapt directly into the side of his body. My left paw struck him directly in his left arm and my right paw grazed his left arm and slid down to his left hip where my claws found a solid surface to grip. I then pushed off and dropped gracefully to all four legs. The impact of my pounce caused the man to drop the paper he was reading; his glasses went flying off his head and fell onto the floor.

The man screamed, "Ow! That hurt!" He grabbed his left arm with his right hand and examined it. "PJ, why did you do that? That hurt!"

The tone of his voice confused me. *You taught me to*

pounce on you before meals and now you raise your voice at me? I thought you would be pleased.

The man reached down and picked up the paper and his eyeglasses. When he straightened back up, he seemed more composed. He stared down at me and softened his expression. "Sharon's right. I did teach you to attack me before feeding you. It's like you're a little Cato and I'm Inspector Clouseau.

I have no idea who you are talking about. But he just kept talking, "Who would have thought that I would be roleplaying a character from the *Pink Panther* with my adopted Weimaraner playing the role of my manservant? One trained to attack in order to keep me alert and my martial arts skills polished."

Yeah, whatever.

He walked into the kitchen. I just stood and stared but did not follow. He stopped at the island in the center of the kitchen and opened a drawer just beneath the cooktop. He pulled out a huge frying pan from the drawer and waved it in my direction. The man laughed out loud. "PJ, this is just for my protection. Now, would you like to have some dinner?"

What a strange man. Does he think I was going to pounce on him a second time? Is that what we practiced together? No, it's not. There's no surprise element. Besides, I didn't like the tone of his voice when I pounced on him in the den. I'm certainly not going to reward his bad behavior. I nonchalantly walked over to the small room where my water and food bowls resided and sat down.

"Okay, girlfriend. I guess you are one and done on your Cato attacks." The man opened the drawer and slid the skillet back inside. He then walked over, picked up my bowl, went to the cabinet and fished out a bag of pellets. As soon as he opened the bag, the aroma of beef wafted through the air.

Oh, I so love that smell. It's almost as good as bacon.

The man returned to the small room and placed the bowl of pellets next to my water bowl. I waited for him to walk away before sniffing the bowl to confirm what I already knew, that this is the same food the man had fed me in the morning. *If you count my meal with the elderly couple, this is my third meal of today. Not a bad day at all.*

*****

The rest of the evening was fairly uneventful. When the woman came home for the evening, she and the man had their dinner. The man behaved himself for the most part. While they were eating, I did overhear something about erecting a doggy fence. The kind and level headed woman quickly talked him out of it.

"You should know by now that PJ is an expert escape artist," she said. "Putting up another doggy fence would just be an exercise in futility. How many broken fences do you want to collect?"

"I suppose you're right," he said.

After dinner, the man and woman went into the den. The man did the nicest thing... he brought my wonderful bed from the back room into the den so I could lay on the floor and watch TV with them. Although the flat screen on the wall looked like a blue haze to me. I was exhausted from all the day's events and fell sound asleep. I woke up when I felt the man's hand on me gently petting my shoulder. I slightly opened my eyes.

The man said, "Well, Cato, have you had enough for today? Would you like to go outside before we all go to bed?"

Why am I now suddenly being called Cato? I believe the name you started with is...PJ. Am I correct? And whatever happened to Mila?

I followed the man over to the door that led to the backyard. My front leg still ached from where it caught on the large gate when I was forced to escape earlier today. Instead of trotting, I walked slowly across the deck and onto the backyard. I did not even stop to sniff for the rabbits. The man waited at the backdoor and pretended not to watch me as I took care of my business. Once I was finished, I walked over and lapped up a bit of fresh water from the big pond. When I turned around, I could see the man shaking his head. However, he did not comment on my need to drink fresh water.

When I entered the den, I noticed that my wonderful

bed was gone. "PJ, let's get some sleep tonight. Do you mind sleeping in your new crate?" We walked together to the back room. My wonderful bed was on one side of the room and my crate, still covered with a blanket, was on the other side underneath the window. I immediately went over to my wonderful bed and made myself comfortable.

The man said, "PJ, let's try out the new crate. Besides, I have a treat to make it worth your while."

This man is all about quid pro quo. But I'm too tired to argue. I stood up and dutifully entered the covered crate for the first time. It was not too bad. *I'll tell you what. If you remove that blanket from on top so I will be able to see daylight come in from the window in the morning, then you have a deal.* The man closed and latched the door. He then extended a beef smelling treat through the crack in the door. I sniffed it and gingerly took it from his hand. *Remember to remove that blanket.* The man did not fulfill his end of the bargain. He ignored my request and walked promptly out of the room, pausing only to switch off the light on his way. *It was a beautiful night, but I was confined and in complete darkness.*

I chewed and swallowed my treat to allow me time to ponder my situation. *I wonder if I can get out of the door? That way I could at least sleep on my wonderful bed and see the stars through the window.* I nudged the door with my muzzle, but it did not budge a bit. I then stroked at it with my right paw. Again, the door did not give. *This is futile. Why couldn't he have secured it with bungee cords? That I can handle. One way or another, I am going to enjoy sleeping where I can see the stars and the first rays of sunshine in the morning.*

I stood up and studied all four sides of the crate. It looked pretty secure. There was only about a two-inch gap between the bars of the crate on all sides, including the roof. I noticed that the blanket covering the crate on the top was ever so slightly penetrating one of the gaps in the bars. I sniffed the blanket and then snipped at it with my left canine tooth. *If only I could get just a small grip.* It took me several tries before I was able to fasten my teeth on the fabric. When I was confident that I had a firm grip, I vigorously snapped my head down. The blanket only gave a few extra inches as it protruded downward through the gap in the roof. Those extra inches were critical because now I could get an even more substantial hold on the blanket with my teeth. Again, I snapped my head down. This time, I made progress in my tug of war with the blanket. It was now penetrating about a foot of fabric through the gap between the crate bars, which no small feat since the gap was only a couple of inches wide.

For the better part of the hour, I followed this same routine of grabbing and then snapping my head. Finally, all but the tail end of the blanket was now inside the crate. The tip of the blanket protruded just above the crate with the remainder of it now resting inside the crate. The appearance of the blanket was almost a mirror reflection of where it was when the man placed it on the crate earlier in the evening. *Should I pull it all the way through? It would take just one final tug. No, I want the man to see the folly of his actions in the morning.* I curled up in a ball in the corner of the crate and glanced up through the gaps in the roof. The moonlight piercing the window above my crate was casting shadows in the room. *What a beautiful night!*

*****

I awoke the next morning with the sunlight streaming in the window above my crate. *Why did the man confine me to the crate all night? I could be up and about by now. No use dwelling on it. I'll just have to wait until the man or woman come and let me out.*

I went back to sleep and did not wake until I heard footsteps on the hardwood floor, approaching my room. When I glanced up, I saw the man standing frozen in the doorway, staring at my crate. He shouted, "You've got to see this!"

From another part of the house, the woman shouted, "See what?"

The man responded, "You will not believe what PJ did overnight!"

The woman joined the man in the doorway to my room. "Last night, I completely covered the crate with that blanket. And look at it now. All but the tail end is now inside! How did she do that?"

The woman laughed. "This is not the first time she has done something to fool you, is it?"

They both walked over to my crate and I stood up and slightly wagged my nub of a tail.

The man asked, "PJ, how did you manage to get that blanket into your crate?"

It was more of a rhetorical question, because I was pretty certain that he didn't really think I was going to respond.

13

Boomer

We were now approaching the end of our trial period in accordance with our adoption agreement. I had not yet made up my mind if I thought this situation was going to be in our mutual best interests. I decided to weigh the pros and cons.

Well, the biggest pro this arrangement has going for it, is the woman. She is caring, sensitive and gentle. As for the man, despite his many flaws, he does have some merit. He gave me a wonderful bed. Also, he gives me a treat every time he eats a meal. And he...well...that's probably all his pros. Now for the cons. The man is conflicted. He is friendly with me one minute and angry the next. He also is slow at times. While he claims to be an attorney, he doesn't know the simple things about contract law. I've never practiced law a day in my life; however, I understand that there are three elements to any bona fide contract: the offer, consideration, and acceptance. The man always forgets that last critical element—acceptance. Even more disturbing is that he fails to follow even the basic provisions of our adoption agreement, which is that I am to have free and full access to the whole house. The man not only does not follow the agreement, but he lacks simple trust. He erects this nonsensical barricade to keep me separated from the rest of the family. How can I trust him if he doesn't trust me? It seems quite elementary to me; he needs to meet me halfway if this arrangement is going to work.

I was so absorbed in my thoughts that I didn't notice the man standing in front of me with a leash in his hand. "Hey girlfriend, are your legs up for a walk?"

Is this a trick? The only time he has used the leash is when we first met and when he retrieved me from the elderly couple's home. I rose to my feet and stretched my legs. When I was appropriately warmed up, I bumped the man's hand that held the leash.

"I'll take that as a 'yes.'"

The man and I walked side by side to the front door. The thought of going for a real walk was exciting. I was getting pumped up. I started prancing in place next to the front door. My prancing did not go unnoticed. "You're kind of excited about this walk, huh?" The man opened the door and he and I walked out onto the front porch. As if he had done this a thousand times, he effortlessly slid the leash over my neck. *This is great! What a beautiful day!*

The man walked slowly through the front yard allowing me to sniff every nook and cranny long the way. We entered the street that ran along the side of the house and headed south. There were all sorts of intriguing smells in the air. A couple of squirrels crossed the street about ten yards ahead of us. *Should I pursue? No, not now. I just want to enjoy walking and exploring.*

The man and I crossed a street and approached a green space. There was only one house to our left, which separated the street that we just crossed and the green space ahead. *I hope the man will let me explore the green space. There's got to be all kinds of scents there.* Just before we reached the green space, we had to pass a wrought iron gate that covered the width of a driveway. As soon as we were even with the gate, we were greeted with loud barking. Both the man and I were startled and jumped slightly in the opposite direction. A big, handsome brown Labrador was behind the gate. He seemed pleased that his barking had startled us. The man said, "Hey Boomer. How are you, big boy? Do you want to say hi to PJ?"

As I stared at the Labrador, it occurred to me that this was the same dog that I had previously seen out the window from the man's room. That time I surprised him and his man by barking at them. *Boy, he's a handsome guy!* I walked over to the gate and the Labrador stuck his nose through one of the bars in the gate. I sniffed his nose and gave him a subtle lick. He wagged his tail and pressed up against the gate. I could tell he was a bit smitten with me. In all honesty, I was a bit smitten with him as well.

The man said, "Now that you've met Boomer let's go check out the green space." As we were walking away, I turned and gave Boomer one last look. Sure enough, he was still staring at me. *The big boy is definitely smitten!*

The man and I walked to the center of the green space and he reached down and slipped the leash over my head. "Why don't you just follow your nose for a while and see where it takes you, PJ?" I did exactly as he suggested and wandered off a bit on my own. The man shouted, "Just don't roll in anything evil. Otherwise, you will get another bath!"

There were all kinds of exciting scents to explore as I made my way through the green space. Periodically, I would glance up to make sure the man was still in sight. He was slowly walking the length of the green space and seemed to be lost in thought. I picked up a scent of what I was certain was a rabbit. Within seconds, I was in full stalking mode. Slowly, I would lift one leg up and then another as I walked through the tall grass that bordered the green space. I was careful not to make too much noise in case my prey was still near. When I glanced up to check on the man, I saw him staring in my direction.

"PJ, come here. I need to hook you back up. There's another dog coming this way."

I looked around and noticed a man and a small dog approaching on the path that led through the green space.

They were about fifty yards from where the man was standing. The man whistled in my direction. *What is it with this whistling?* When I did not immediately respond, the man shouted "PJ! Please come here!" *Well, since he asked politely, I will oblige him.* I trotted over to him and stopped a few feet away. I must have brushed up against something in the tall grass because I had a sudden need to scratch my left ear. As I was taking care of my itch, the man approached me and slipped the collar over my head. I could feel the coldness of the metal choker around my neck.

The other man and small dog were now only a few feet away. The other man wore a maroon colored shirt with the printing "Texas A&M" on his chest. The man said to the other man, "How do you think the Aggies are going to do this year in the S.E.C.?"

The other man smiled and said, "No telling. Not sure anyone is going to get by Alabama. Are you an Aggie?"

The man chuckled out loud. "Far from it! I went to U.T."

The other man smiled and responded, "Well, we can't all be fortunate to be Aggies, I guess."

The man said, "That's true, but there have got to be some Longhorns, too!" Both men then struck up a conversation about missing the Big 12 rivalry and other such nonsense. Meanwhile, the small dog seemed to be oblivious to everything. He had curled up at the other man's feet and was nearly asleep.

What is it with these guys? No one is paying any attention to me. I would much rather be exploring the green space than listening to two old guys lament about meaningless history. By the time they began to talk about the old Southwest Conference, I knew that it was time to do what I do best. I began to chew on the cord of the leash. With my left Canine tooth firmly clinched on the leash, I began to gnaw. After only a few minutes, I had completely severed the leash. My actions had gone undetected. I rose to my feet and glanced upwards at the two men. They were completely absorbed in their conversation.

Where to go first? Should I go back to the tall grass? On the other hand, maybe I should go get better acquainted with Boomer.

I swiftly retreated back down the green space to the corner house that backed up to the green space. Before leaving the green space, I shot a glance around at the man. From this distance I could barely hear him shouting, "PJ! PJ! Where are you?" *Now, you want to know where I am. What about ten minutes ago?*

I stepped into the street and walked up to the wrought iron gate and stuck my nose through one of the openings. I could smell Boomer, but I could not see him. *Maybe if I whimper a bit, it will get his attention.* I walked back and forth along the fence rubbing the side of my body on the iron slats. *If Boomer is not outside, he will certainly know that I have been here.* I was about to give up and leave, when I heard the garage door open. A black car started to back out of the garage onto the driveway. There was Boomer standing in the middle of the garage watching the car back out. I heard a man's voice from the driver's side of the car say, "Boomer, you stay in the garage now."

Boomer stood motionless, staring at the black car. The wrought iron gate then started to open at the same time as the garage door was lowering. The motion of the gate opening caught Boomer's attention. He then noticed that I was standing there and staring at him. I watched as Boomer just cleared the closing garage door, bounding onto the driveway in my direction.

Now, that I have his attention, what am I going to do with him? I sprinted down the street towards my house, but took a sharp right in front of Boomer's house and continued down the street. Boomer in pursuit just barely maneuvered through the opening in the wrought iron gate. The man in the black car started shouting, "Boomer, where are you going? Come back here!"

After going a few more yards down the street, I paused to look back over my shoulder. There was Boomer, rounding the corner of his house at a dead run. There were several large ceramic potted plants that separated the front of Boomer's house from the side yard. In the excitement of the chase, Boomer forgot about these large potted plants. He attempted to hurdle them at the last second. Instead, he crashed like a bowling ball, knocking down all three. There was the unmistakable sound of ceramic breaking on impact with concrete. Boomer seemed stunned as he stood in the mayhem that he had just created. The black car then rounded the corner and came to a screeching halt in front of Boomer's house. The man exited the car and slammed the door shut. Even from where I was positioned, I could tell he was very agitated. He walked briskly over to where Boomer was standing. "Boomer, you're in big trouble! Look, what you've done!" The man roughly grabbed Boomer by the collar and led him back around the house.

That was close. I don't think the man driving the car ever saw me. It's time to go and find the man.

I retraced my steps to the street that ran alongside Boomer's house and intersected the green space. When I rounded the corner, I saw the man talking to the man who had driven the black car near the wrought iron gate, which was now closed. The man asked, "What was that noise? I thought I heard glass breaking."

The man with the black car responded, "That was Boomer. For some inexplicable reason, he went running out of my gate when I was trying to back my car out. You know those huge ceramic planters that my wife adores; the ones at the front corner of my house?"

The man nodded his head.

"Well, that was the crash that you heard. Boomer flattened them as he ran around the corner at a dead run. He's usually reasonably well behaved. I cannot fathom what caused him to act that way. It was like he was possessed and intent on catching something."

When I approached the two men, the man said, "PJ, where have you been?"

The man with the black car asked, "So, is this your new dog?"

The man responded, "Yes, we just adopted her a few days ago. We're still getting acquainted with each other. While I was talking to some guy in the green space, PJ chewed through her leash and escaped. The man held up the pieces of the severed leash as he spoke. "She's quite the escape artist. I am just so glad she didn't get lost or cause any problems for someone."

The man with the black car leaned down and patted me on the head. You're a pretty girl. You wouldn't cause any problems for anybody would you?"

I could smell Boomer on his hands. *I wonder what the man with the black car did with Boomer?*

The man crudely tied the two severed pieces of leash together and attached it to my collar. He said to the man with the black car, "So sorry about your planters. Give my best to your wife and Boomer."

The man with the black car smiled. "Boomer is going to get something. But I assure you, it won't be anyone's best."

The man and I walked back down the street towards the man's house. *I wonder what's for dinner tonight? Will it be those same beef-like smelling pellets or will the man come up with something a little more creative?*

14

Playing Opposum

On my fourth day with the man and woman, the woman stayed at home with the man. Usually, she left early in the morning and returned in the evening. On the other hand, the man would stay at home all day staring at the monitor and periodically tapping his fingers on the computer keyboard. The woman typically woke up early and gave me her full attention until I had taken care of my morning business. Even though she fed me the same boring food as the man, she had a kind and gentle way to her. She talked softly to me as she was preparing my breakfast. She did not expect any of the nonsense that the man expected when he practically insisted that I attack him in order to be fed. Once my needs were addressed, she would prepare her own breakfast and ready herself for the day somewhere outside of the house. I did not know why she left every morning. However, I knew after a few days that she would always return in the evening.

After preparing my breakfast, the man and woman ate their breakfast. I positioned myself between the kitchen and the dining room and laid down.

While the man had his faults, he did keep one promise to me. He always saved something off his plate to give me before washing the dishes. We were quickly developing a ritual. As soon as the man pushed back his chair from the dining table, I would rise to my feet and wait for the man to pick up his plate and then the woman's plate. Then as soon as he walked passed me, I would follow right behind him into the kitchen where he would set his plate next to the sink and hand me a morsel of food off his plate. This morning it was bacon. *Good choice! Why don't you feed me bacon for breakfast instead of the beef-smelling pellets?*

I waited in the kitchen until the man washed the dishes. *I wonder if he is always going to just give me one morsel of food off his plate following a meal. If I hang around long enough, maybe he will get the idea that two or three morsels off his plate would be much better.* The man seemed oblivious to my presence as he methodically washed the dishes. *He is obviously not going to give me any more food. I better check on the woman to see what she is up to.*

I left the man in the kitchen and trotted back to the man and woman's bedroom. When I arrived, the woman was lacing up her shoes. I walked up and sniffed her shoes.

All kinds of fascinating scents, including grass and perspiration. These must be special shoes.

When she finished tying her shoes, she stood up and said, "Girlfriend, do you want to go for a walk?"

A walk? You bet I'm interested. Let's go.

The man then entered the bedroom and said, "You ready to take the girl for a walk?"

The woman responded, "We're all ready. I'll get the leash from the closet while you get ready. The woman exited the bedroom and I followed her. She walked over to the closet in the den and opened the door. I heard the unmistakable sound of a leash. *Yes, I heard correctly! We're definitely going for a walk!* I started prancing in circles around the woman as she made her way to the front door. I was so excited that I could barely contain myself.

She stopped at the front door and patted my head. "I know you're excited but we have to wait for daddy."

Who is this daddy character?

"Here he is."

The man walked through the living room and over to the front door. He said, "One rule before we go, PJ! Don't chew through the leash. I had a hard time tying this one back together."

The man opened the door and the three of us walked outside. *I hope we are going to Boomer's house!* Sure enough, the three of us walked down the street that bordered the man's house, heading towards Boomer's house and the green space. The woman was holding my leash. I continued to prance and jerk on the end of the leash to try and hurry the man and woman along. *Don't they know how anxious I am to see Boomer?*

Thirty yards, twenty yards, we were almost to the wrought iron gate. I glanced over and noticed the remaining remnants of the potted plants and ceramic containers that Boomer crashed through the previous evening. *We're almost there.*

The choker collar tightened around my neck as I kept pulling and trying to influence the direction we were going. The man said, "PJ met Boomer last night. I think that's why she is pulling you towards the wrought iron gate."

The woman responded, "She must have liked seeing Boomer." She gave me some slack in the leash and I walked over to the gate. There was no sign of Boomer anywhere. *I wonder if the man with the black car took Boomer somewhere? I'd better rub up against the slats in the gate so he will know that I've been here.*

The man said, "Look at her. She's leaving her scent for Boomer. Isn't that sweet?"

The man and the woman allowed me to rub up several times on the gate before the woman gave me a slight tug on the leash. *Okay, okay, I'm coming.* The man, woman, and I made a left just beyond Boomer's house onto the green space. The three of us walked along the path of the green space. I could smell all kinds of scents emanating from the grass and weeds that surrounded the path. *I wish the woman would let me off the leash so I can explore. Regardless, I enjoy being outside.*

We followed the pathway for about a mile, crossing two streets along the way. About a hundred yards after crossing the second street, the woman reached down and slipped the leash over my head "Okay, PJ, go have some fun." Directly in front of me was a cluster of tall grass and heavy brush. *That is where I am going first.* I sprinted into the center of the brush out of the sight of the man and woman.

I immediately froze. *What's that smell? I know cat, squirrel, and rabbit scents, but this is something altogether different. Time to go into stalking mode.* I carefully sniffed the entire periphery of where I was standing without picking up a stronger scent. Just when I was about to give up, there was a slight disturbance in some tall grass to my right. I cautiously moved in the direction of the disturbance. *Front right foot up, left rear foot down. My movement must go undetected.* I repeated this classic stalking mode for several minutes until I came across a slight clearing in the tall grass. Lying in the middle of the clearing was the source of what was causing the strong scent. I moved slowly and deliberately right up to the grayish brown object.

It was completely motionless. I sniffed and then nudged it slightly with my nose. Still, the object did not move. Instinctively, I reached down and clasped my teeth gently but firmly around it, and raised it off the ground and set it back down. Suddenly, it squirmed and rose to its feet. When I reached down again and clinched it with my teeth, it emitted some foul smelling fluid. *I need to show the man and woman what I found.* With this smelly object firmly clasped in my teeth, I ran back through the brush to the spot where I remembered last seeing the man and woman.

The foul smelling fluid was becoming overbearing. The woman said, "Look, she has something in her mouth!"

The man responded, "I think it's an opossum! PJ, drop it!"

He did not have to ask twice. The opossum's foul smelling fluid was making me nauseated. I unclenched my teeth and dropped the opossum. It hit the ground and ran back towards the cluster of tall grass and immediately disappeared. I was coughing, sneezing and spitting all at the same time. Nothing I did could get that awful taste out of my mouth. I began to drool and froth at the mouth.

The woman said, "Oh my, what's wrong with her?"

The man replied, "The opossum must have some kind of defense mechanism that releases an odor. Whatever it was didn't agree with PJ."

The woman slipped the leash back over my head and said, "PJ, let's go home and check you out."

We began the walk along on the path back towards the man and woman's house. Every two or three yards, I would pause to wipe my face against the grass that bordered the path to try and get some relief. Nonetheless, I continued to froth uncontrollably. About a quarter of the way home, there was a woman and a small boy approaching us on the pathway. When we were only a few yards away the boy shouted, "Look, mommy, that dog has rabies!" The woman grabbed the boy by the shoulders and ushered him off the pathway. With a horrified look on her face she asked, "What's wrong with your dog?"

The man paused and said, "She got tangled up with an opossum. I am sure she's fine." The woman seemed unconvinced and stood several yards to the side of the path while we walked passed. She was shielding the boy as if to protect him from contracting rabies from the "unfortunate dog." After walking a few more yards, I glanced over my shoulder. The woman and boy were still standing and staring in our direction.

We continued on our way down the path. I still could not get that bitter, nauseating taste out of my mouth. A few yards ahead, an elderly man was slowly approaching us. He would take a few steps and then pause to rest and lean on his right hand, which firmly clutched a cane. After a few moments, he would take another step or two and then follow the same routine. When the man, woman, and I were only a several feet away, he just stood and stared at me. Instead of taking a few more steps, he raised his cane and pointed it in my direction. The man with the cane said, "That dog of yours don't look right. She's foaming at the mouth like she's got rabies."

The man grimaced and responded, "She doesn't have rabies!" I could tell by the tone of his voice that he was tired of responding to questions about my health.

The man with the cane said, "If you say so. I got to tell

you though, son, I ain't seen anything like that since I was a boy on the farm in East Texas. We had a lot of dogs that got mixed up with the wrong company and came down with rabies. I've had to shoot one or two myself."

This time the woman responded, "She just got mixed up with an opossum. She will be fine." She grabbed the man's arm and said, "Let's get PJ home."

The man, woman, and I walked hurriedly passed the man with a cane. He was continuing to murmur, "That sure looks like rabies."

Finally, we were almost at the start of the green space near Boomer's house. The woman asked, "You don't think it is possible that PJ has rabies do you?"

The man sighed heavily, "No, the opossum just did a number on her. Besides, you don't just immediately start foaming at the mouth when you contract rabies."

She asked, "How do you know so much about rabies?"

The man chuckled. "Well, I guess I've seen the movie *Old Yeller* a dozen or so times, so I'm pretty much an expert on when dogs start showing the signs of rabies."

The man and woman both laughed out loud. By this time, I was starting to feel better. The bitter taste had almost completely subsided. By the time we reached Boomer's house, I felt almost normal. *I wonder if he is outside?* Just the thought of possibly seeing Boomer makes me feel really perky. When we arrived at the location of the street that was even with Boomer's wrought iron gate, I snuck a furtive glance to see if he were there. *Shoot, he's nowhere in sight. What has the man in the black car done with him? Just because he broke a few planters doesn't mean he should be imprisoned inside his house.* The couple and I walked the last couple of blocks until we were at the man and woman's house.

Once we were inside, I immediately ran through the house to the backdoor in the den. *I need to get some fresh water and rinse my mouth.* The man walked over and opened the door for me. He stood at the backdoor and watched as I sprinted out to pond in the backyard. I lapped water for several seconds. *It feels good to get that taste out of my mouth.* When I was finished drinking, I trotted back to the house and bounded onto to the deck.

The man greeted me on my return, "Why do you insist on drinking out of my pool when you have fresh water in the house?" By the tone of his voice, I knew he wasn't angry with me. *Never mind. I'll go lie down on my bed and rest a bit. All the excitement with that critter in the green space has taken its toll on me.* I trotted to the back room and over to my bed. After circling a few requisite times on it, I plopped down for a nap. I do not know how long I slept.

*****

I woke up to the sound of the man and woman walking through the kitchen towards my room. When they entered my room, the man stopped in front of the steel dog crate. "Come on, girlfriend, let's lock you up. We have to run some errands."

I reluctantly rose to my feet and stepped off my bed. *Time to stretch.* I extended my front paws forward as far they could go followed by my hind legs. *Why do you always feel it necessary to lock me in the crate when you leave? If you want me to trust you, you need to trust me as well.* I walked over and slowly entered the crate.

The man reached down and started to latch the door behind me. He paused and said, "PJ, I know you've had a traumatic day with the opossum and all. Can I trust you not to destroy our new den rug or get on the sofa while we are gone?" I sat in my crate and stared up at the man. "For better or worse, I am going leave your crate open." He then handed me a beef-smelling treat. I did not immediately take it from his hand so he placed it just inside the door of the crate. He stood up and said to the woman, "You ready to go?"

She smiled and responded, "Sure! I'm just surprised that you trust PJ not to destroy the house while we are gone."

The man sighed, "Well, she has been with us almost a week now. I guess we should find out if we can trust her or not."

I waited silently in the crate until the man and woman left the house. When I was certain that they were gone, I reached down and clenched the treat with my teeth. *It was thoughtful of the man to give me a treat without confining me against my will.*

I quickly consumed the treat and spun around three times in the crate before plopping down. *This bedding is not too shabby. Somehow, it seems downright comfortable now that I know I can leave anytime that I wish. Time for a nap!*

15

From Tortilla Thief to Best Friend

———

I woke up on the final day of the trial period under my adoption agreement with the man and woman. My first thoughts, however, were not about the adoption agreement, but about the noise just outside the window of my room. I took a step off of my bed and performed my obligatory stretch to get my legs warmed up after a long night. A couple of shakes of my ears and I was ready to go and check on the noise and take care of my business. I trotted into the kitchen and smelled the aroma of coffee. *I am not sure why the man and woman started every single day with a cup of coffee. For me, I would rather skip right to the bacon.*

When I walked into the den, I saw the man in the backyard talking to some other men who were all dressed in white. The man was pointing at the eaves of the house and talking while the other men stood around and nodded their heads. I walked over to the back door of the den and scratched the wood part of the door with my right paw. The sound got the man's attention. He stopped pointing at the eaves and walked across the deck and opened the back door. I immediately sprinted by him to go check out the men dressed in white.

The man called to the men dressed in white, "Don't worry she's very friendly."

The men dressed in white just stood and stared as I sniffed their shoes and pants. The man joined us back under the eaves and asked, "So, is this a one-day job to paint the eaves on the back of the house?"

The oldest of the men dressed in white responded, "Yes, that shouldn't be any problem at all. In fact, we should be done by mid-afternoon."

The man said, "Great! I'll go inside and let you guys get to work."

While the man was walking back to the door of the den, I was finishing up my morning business on a green patch of grass next to the pond in the backyard. Once I was done, I trotted over to the pond to get a drink of fresh water. When I looked back up after lapping up a little bit of water, I noticed the man staring at me from inside the back door. He was smiling and shaking his head back and forth. I ran passed the men dressed in white and bounded up onto the deck and towards the house. When I was a few feet from the back door, the man opened the door for me. I trotted by him and into the kitchen.

The woman had my food bowl on the counter and was pouring beef-smelling pellets into it. She smiled at me when she saw me. "Are you hungry, sweet girl?" I wagged my nub of a tail in response. The woman crossed the kitchen with my bowl and gently set it in the small room next to a bowl of water.

It took less than a few minutes for me to consume all of my breakfast. *I'd better go check on the man and woman.* As I entered the hall, I could hear the man tapping on the keyboard. I did not even have to go all the way there to know that he was sitting at his desk staring into the monitor. Instead, I entered the man and woman's bedroom and joined the woman in her large closet. She appeared to be in the process of selecting her shoes. I spied the shoes that she had worn on our walk yesterday.

Time is of the essence. I need to influence her decision. If she selects the same shoes she wore yesterday, maybe she will take me by Boomer's house and to the green space. I reared up on my hind legs and nudged the shoes from yesterday with my nose, causing one of them to fall to the ground.

The woman laughed out loud. "You're trying to convince me to take you on a walk, aren't you?" She leaned over and patted my head. "Sorry, girlfriend. I've got to go to work. Maybe you can convince the old grumpy guy to take you instead." I sat down and watched patiently as she picked up her shoe from yesterday and returned it to the shelf. *I guess that means we're not going to the green space.* The woman then selected a different pair of shoes and slipped them on. I walked over and sniffed them. *No interesting smells like the other shoes.*

I followed the woman back out of the bedroom and into the room where the man was sitting and staring at the monitor. When we entered, he flipped around in his chair. "You off to work?"

The woman responded, "Yes, I'm already running late."

I walked over and curled up on some bedding that the man had placed on the floor next to his desk. The woman gave the man a kiss and walked back towards the hallway. Without looking back, she paused and said, "By the way, this is the final day of our trial period under the adoption agreement with PJ. If I were you, I'd take her for a walk. I think you need all the points you can get."

The man laughed. "You're right. This is the final day. Are we going to love her or return her?"

The woman turned back around and sighed. "If you take her back, you might as well not come back yourself."

The man replied, "I thought that might be your position. However, I will say this. If we had not adopted her, we would've saved a couple of thousand dollars on a rug and damaged blinds." He gestured towards the gap in the blinds bearing my teeth marks.

Always finding a positive to everything, the woman responded, "That's true, but look how she's come around.

At first, she's stealing cheese and look at her now. She's perfectly content to curl up next to her daddy."

The man playfully groaned. "I am certainly no daddy!" He continued, "Those first few days were brutal. It was like she was inflicting pain on us for keeping her confined. On the other hand, the agreement did say she'd have full run of the house. I didn't interpret that to mean 24/7 though."

The woman smiled. "Well, apparently she had her own interpretation."

As the woman started to walk away, the man shouted, "Punitive damages!"

Just down the hallway, she shouted back, "What are punitive damages?"

"They are damages rarely awarded in a breach of contract cases and only under egregious circumstances," the man replied.

While walking down the hallway towards the den, the woman responded, "Wouldn't you consider being locked up against your will for hours on end in a small bathroom pretty egregious?"

The man shouted back, "She obviously did!"

Barely audible, the woman shouted, "Have a good day!"

The man shouted towards the direction of the doorway, "You too!"

I hope this talk means that I get to go visit Boomer and the green space.

The man continued to stare at the monitor and

occasionally tap his fingers on the keyboard. *Time for a little nap.* I dozed off and spent the better part of the morning lying next to the man's desk. Occasionally, he would get up and walk out the door from his room that led to the side of the yard. Each time, I would follow him out and sniff around a bit. It was a beautiful day. Around noon, we heard a tap at the man's door.

The man got up, walked over, and cracked open the door. He said, "How are things going?"

The oldest of the men dressed in white was standing just outside. He responded, "Fine. We're going to take a break and go get some lunch. Do you mind if we bring it back and eat at the table out there by your pool?"

The man responded, "Not a problem at all. Help yourself." He closed the door, and looked down at me. "PJ, I think I'm going to get some lunch too." The man walked to the kitchen with me close behind. In my short time here, I always tried to take advantage of opportunities to be in the kitchen when food is involved. *The man may want to give me a treat.* The man quickly assembled some wonderful smelling meats and placed them between two pieces of bread. He then grabbed a paper towel and began to walk back towards his room. *What? Nothing for me?* We made eye contact and he paused. "PJ, as always I promise to save part of my lunch for you." *I have to admit that the man has been pretty consistent when it came to promises of food.*

The man methodically consumed his sandwich while he sat at his desk and stared at the monitor. Periodically, he would set down his sandwich and tap his fingers on the keyboard. When he was down to a solitary bite, he looked down at me. "Here, PJ!" The man tossed his remaining sandwich in my direction. I caught it like a center fielder catching a baseball. He asked, "How can you be so adept at catching a sandwich, but completely clueless when it comes to catching a ball?"

You're starting to ramble and I want to go outside. I walked over to the door that led outside and scratched the door with my right paw. The man arose from his chair and opened the door for me. I bounded out into the side yard and around to the pond. When I arrived the men dressed in white were seated at the large table near the pond. Two men were seated on one side facing the pond and the other man was seated at the other end of the table. They did not pay any attention to me as I sniffed a bit around in the garden next to the concrete deck by the pond. *That smells good!* The scent of food was drifting over from the table. *What's that smell?* I couldn't readily identify it. I stood motionless and sniffed the air. The man sitting by himself at the end of the table said, "Damn, I left my soda in the truck." He stood up and started walking towards the side of the yard, which led to the gate at the front of the fence. I waited as he disappeared around the corner of the house before I moved. In full stalk mode, I crept slowly through the garden and onto the concrete deck. One step and then another. I was just below the end of the table where the man dressed in white had previously been seated. The other two men dressed in white were talking and eyeing the pond. I reared up and in one quick precise action grabbed the food off a paper plate.

I had my prize clenched securely in my teeth and I silently retraced my steps through the garden and found a comfortable spot in the grass just out of sight of the table. None of the men dressed in white appeared to observe my actions. *This is tasty. Wow, this is real beef inside some kind of crispy delicious wrapping.* Before I could finish off the crispy beef thing, I heard the man dressed in white, the one who had left the table earlier shout, "Hey man, who stole my tortilla?"

The other two men dressed in white started laughing. The oldest man dressed in white said, "We didn't steal anything. We've been here the whole time eating and staring at the pool."

The man at the end of the table said, "Well, it sure as hell didn't walk off by itself." He stood up and looked around and spotted me licking my chops across the garden. "Did you let that damn dog eat off my plate?"

The other men dressed in white laughed again. "The older man dressed in white responded, "We didn't see a thing. If that dog stole your tortilla, she's a damn good thief."

The man dressed in white at the end of the table started walking in my direction. I could tell by the expression on his face that he was angry. *I'd better get out of here.* Before he reached me, I stood up and started trotting towards the side yard. When I glanced over my shoulder, I could see him running behind me, waving his hands and shouting, "Come back here!"

I accelerated into a run. Easily distancing myself from the angry man dressed in white, I raced up to the door that led to the man's room. I nudged it with my nose but it was firmly shut. When I looked back the angry man dressed in white was drawing near to me. He was close enough that I could see that his face was beet red. I turned around and scratched the door with my front claws. *Please let me in!* When there was no response, I tried a second and then a third time.

The angry man dressed in white was now within a few feet of me. Suddenly, the door swung open. From inside his room the man said, "What's wrong, girlfriend?" Without hesitation, I leapt into the room and ran by the man over to my bedding next to his desk. The man was now face-to-face with the angry man dressed in white. "Is there a problem?"

The angry man dressed in white was breathing heavily, probably from all his running. In between deep breaths, he said, "Yes! You're damn dog stole a tortilla off my plate!"

The man looked over at me. I could see a slight smile form on his face. *What's the man going to do? Is he going to turn me over to the angry man dressed in white?* The man turned back around and faced the angry man dressed in white. "I'm so sorry. How do you suppose she stole a tortilla from you? Did you see her steal it?"

The angry man dressed in white responded, "No. No one saw her. I forgot my soda in my truck. When I came back, my tortilla was gone."

The man sighed. "Were the other two guys still at the table when you left?"

The angry man in white replied, "Yes, they were there. But they said they didn't hear or see anything."

The man calmly said, "So, you just assumed that my dog stole your tortilla right under the noses of your co-workers." *I knew that the man knew I had indeed stolen the tortilla. He was using his lawyer skills to defend me.*

The angry man in white stammered a bit, "Yes, but I saw her licking her chops."

The man scratched his bald head. "Well, one thing is for certain, I'm pretty sure that PJ's not going to confess to anything. So, I'll tell you what I'm going to do. Would you accept twenty dollars for your missing tortilla?"

The angry man dressed in white suddenly became less angry. He flashed a smile. "Are you serious?"

The man responded, "That seems like reasonable damages for your loss. Wait here just a moment." The man left the room and walked down the hallway.

The formerly angry man dressed in white stared down at me. I groaned and closed my eyes. *I have no idea why this guy is staring at me.* The man returned with a twenty-dollar bill and handed it to the formerly angry man dressed in white. "Thanks, Mister!"

The man responded, "You're most welcome. Sorry for your trouble."

The man shut the door and walked back to his desk and sat in his chair. He looked down at me. "PJ, by my estimate, you've cost us fifteen hundred and twenty dollars in just a week since you've been with us."

I stared at the man.

A small price to pay for learning a valuable lesson on trust and a little contract law along the way, wouldn't you say?

The man seemed to understand my thoughts. "You know, PJ, this is the last day of the trial period in our agreement. I've made up my mind about whether to continue this relationship. Have you?"

I stood up on my bed so I could be near the man and put my right paw on his leg. He patted my head. The adoption agreement was binding.

CPSIA information can be obtained
at www.ICGtesting.com
Printed in the USA
LVOW04s1737021216

515533LV00009B/532/P